IONA

A History of the Island

IONA
A History of the Island

Dennis Hardley

F. Marian McNeill

Foreword by the Earl of Wemyss and March

LOCHAR PUBLISHING•MOFFAT•SCOTLAND

First published in 1920 by Blackie & Son Limited.

The Publishers wish to thank the Iona Cathedral Trust for help in providing new and revised material for this edition, Maxwell MacLeod for providing the final chapter and Hugh Webster of The Highland Scene Photograph Library for help with illustrations.

This seventh edition published in 1991 by Lochar Publishing Limited, Moffat, DG10 9ED, Scotland.

British Library Cataloguing in Publication Data

McNeill, F. Marian (Florence Marian) *1885–19*73
   Iona: a history of the island. – 7th ed.
   1. Scotland. Strathclyde Region. Iona to 1991
   I. Title
   941. 423

   ISBN 0–948403–63–2

Typeset in Bembo Monophoto 12 on 14 point by Chapterhouse Limited, The Cloisters, Formby L37 3PX

Printed in Scotland by Eagle Colour Books Ltd.

Map by David Langworth

CONTENTS

To
Helen Weir Mickel
who first directed my steps to Iona

FOREWORD

There is something very special about Iona. Numerous people have said so, and countless thousands throughout the ages have been consciously or unconsciously influenced by its special quality. Many and various have been the writers who have expressed this feeling in prose and poem and the original edition of this book was certainly an outstanding example. Doubtless the feeling that 'God is in this place' stems from the residence there of Columcille – Saint Columba – whose personality and whose community had a widespreading and enduring influence, political as well as religious. But even before the Saint's arrival, with his twelve companions, in 563 it seems that this modest but beautiful island was in some sense a sacred place of the Druids of the ancient religion. It is even believed that these worshippers of the sun were consciously waiting some further revelation, and that the famous encircled Celtic Cross represents the sun's disc supporting and completed by the plain cross of the Christian redemption.

Iona – under its proper name of Í, more fully I Chaluim Chille certainly became an important centre of the celtic-Irish type of Christianity, and a focus from which the Gospel spread, primarily to the more northern parts of Caledonia. (The island lay on the borderline between Scots and Picts) and became 'the luminary of the Caledonian Regions'. Its influence soon extended to central and southern parts of Scotland and deep into English lands. With constant cross-fertilisation and with their Irish origins the missionaries from this furthest edge of the Atlantic spread far and wide over Europe, to the Alps and beyond, where monasteries and seats of learning began to herald a reviving civilisation.

I still vividly remember my first visit, at the age of fourteen, on the old *Dunara Castle*, famous in her day along with her sister ship *Hebrides* as the cargo and tourist lifeline of all these western parts. These two ships maintained the only regular connection with St. Kilda; and had I remained on board instead of disembarking on South Uist I would have seen St. Kilda an inhabited place – for that year, 1926, was the last but four for that unique and remote community. But Iona was, for me, sufficient reward. The *Dunara Castle* remained most of the day at anchor in the Sound, while shore boats plied to and fro. So deeply impressed was I with the atmosphere of the place, the Abbey and Village in view, and the low hills behind, that I remained in contemplation all day and never got ashore!

In numerous visits since that long ago time I have always found deep satisfaction and growing interest: and it was indeed a happy thing when, in 1979, through the generosity of the Fraser Foundation, the island came into the ownership of the National Trust for Scotland. The Trust's ownership could be called a 'background' situation, because it excludes numerous houses and public buildings, the attractive Parish Chruch and Manse, two of the crofts, and in particular the Abbey and other religious buildings. These last belong since 1899 to the Cathedral Trust set up by the 8th Duke of Argyll; a fine ecumenical action in its time, since the buildings were specifically made available to all Christian denominations. Since then the Cathedral Trust has completed the restoration of the Abbey Church, largely achieved by the Duke before the handing over, and seen the re-building of the cloisters and monastic buildings, with which the name of George MacLeod will always be gratefully associated. In recent years I have been privileged to join the Cathedral Trust's Management Board, and seen much good work carried out on these very special buildings by our permanent squad of local men, and many promising developments in their better display and interpretation.

I hope and pray that the background presence of the National Trust for Scotland will continue to give a sense of security to all who know and love this very special island, to the ninety or so people who live and work there, and to those whose particular care is the maintenance and enhancement of this great heritage of buildings, and the religious life and exploration there centred.

THE EARL OF WEMYSS AND MARCH (*lately*) *President of the National Trust for Scotland*

PREFACE

'When I visited Iona in 1917,' the author wrote in her first preface, 'I tried to obtain a modest handbook which should give a concise and comprehensive account of the island; its history and significance in the progress of our Western civilisation; its antiquities of the Celtic and mediaeval periods; and, not least, its folk-lore, which gives life and colour to almost every nook and cranny on the little island . . . I have tried here to compile the book I vainly sought, and trust it will meet the need which many others have felt.'

In 1917 only the Abbey church among the venerable ruins redolent of Iona's part in fourteen centuries of Christian history had been restored. The High Cross of St. John, now recognised as one of the glories of British art and erected again on Iona in 1990, was a heap of broken stone and a stump of shaft which had yet to be matched again. The Iona Community, whose members restore the monastic buildings and are now custodians of an Abbey complex bustling with cheerful activity, was not even a dream in the mind of its founder, the young Captain George MacLeod on active service in France.

The first edition appeared in 1920. In the seventy years since then, the outpouring of books and articles about Iona, of varying quality, has continued apace. A substantial vehicle-carrying ferryboat has replaced the small launch that used to bring visitors across from Fionnphort, and the old round-Mull steamer that once dropped anchor at Iona no longer sails. The number of visitors approaches 140,000 a year, and these seventy years may have seen more visitors than the previous thirteen centuries since St. Columba chose Iona for his monastery.

Scholarly knowledge of the island and of Celtic culture has much expanded too. But the flavour of this little classic survives, and in bringing up to date its factual material and contemporary description, the publishers have been careful to preserve that essential resonance that has charmed so many readers over the years.

Dennis Hardley

*I*ona Abbey and the village adorn the sandy shores of the much visited island.

Dennis Hardley

A summer view of the Iona/Mull ferry looking across the Sound of Mull towards Iona's eastern shore – the Abbey can be seen in the background.

Chapter One

INTRODUCTION

In the midst of the Hebrides or Western Isles of Scotland lies a little island, fashioned of rock and heather, on which the Atlantic seas beat ceaselessly. So small and modest is its aspect, so indistinguisable amongst its myriad sister isles, that the traveller who has not fully learned the secret of its spell may well marvel at its power to draw and hold the homage of men of many lands and creeds and centuries.

Fourteen hundred years ago, on the last day of his life, St. Columba, whose name is forever bound with that of Iona, ascended the little hill overlooking the monastery, and blessed the island, saying:

> *Unto this place, small and mean though it be, great homage shall yet be paid, not only by the kings and peoples of the Scots, but by the rulers of barbarous and distant nations with their people. Thy saints also, of other churches, shall regard it with no common reverence.*

This prophecy has been remarkably fulfilled. And not only did the centuries provide a continuous stream of travellers from over the civilized world, but for many generations the bodies of princes and chiefs were brought hither to lie in its hallowed soil. The procession of the dead has long since ceased, but still the pilgrims come.

To the traveller, who would not let the glamour and significance of Iona escape him, as they escape many, it is well to emphasize that he will find no stimulus to his imagination in wild, awe-inspiring scenery or imposing array of ancient ruins. Natural beauty the island assuredly possesses, but it is a beauty so demure, so winsome, that it is apt to evade those whose taste inclines to a more exotic type. But for those who have eyes to see, there is a subtle beauty in the apparent barrenness: a beauty mainly of atmosphere: a beauty part physical, part spiritual.

Although lacking the grandeur of conception and luxuriance of setting boasted by great ecclesiastical centres elsewhere, the devotedly restored Abbey buildings and the beautiful remains of the Nunnery on Iona show to the initiated a rare beauty of design and skilled workmanship. The marvellous carving of the high crosses testifies to the antiquity of artistry on the island, at a time in the eighth century for which surviving records and artefacts are scanty. The two flowerings of Iona's sculpture, in early Christian times and in the Middle Ages, justify their wide renown and cannot but inspire wonder in the modern traveller that somewhere so remote, so ill provided with the materials and machines on which modern man depends, should produce memorials of such beauty.

The attitude of mind of the voyager to Iona is all-important, and for that he must know something of its place in the spiritual history of the world. 'Let us approach that sacred isle,' writes Bishop Ewing, 'with more than common reverence: there where it now lies in the midst of rolling billows, and listening but to sea-birds' cries, from age to age in the morning of early history, night and day it heard the sweet songs of God.'

'Since the remotest days,' writes Fiona Macleod, 'sacrosanct men have bowed here in worship. In this little isle a lamp was lit whose flame lighted pagan Europe ... Here Learning and Faith had their tranquil home, when the shadow of the sword lay upon all lands ... From age to age lowly hearts have never ceased to bring their burden there.'

Even Dr. Johnson, that sturdy Saxon and unlikely pilgrim to such a spot, was moved to write about Iona:

We are now treading that illustrious isle which was once the luminary of the Caledonian regions, whence savage clans and moving barbarians derived the benefits of knowledge and the blessings of religion. To abstract the mind from all local emotion would be impossible if it were endeavoured, and would be foolish if it were possible. Whatever withdraws us from the power of our senses, whatever makes the past, the distant, or the future predominate over the present, advances us in the dignity of thinking beings. Far from me and my friends be such frigid philosophy as may conduct us, indifferent and unmoved, over any ground which has been dignified by wisdom, bravery or virtue. That man is little to be envied whose patriotism would not gain force upon the plains of Marathon, or whose piety would not grow warmer among the ruins of Iona.

Iona is a very small island – about three miles long and one or more in breadth – situated off the west coast of Argyllshire, and separated from the south-west coast of Mull by a narrow sound about half a mile across. It has a lovely setting in the blue Hebridean seas, which stretch, island-studded, to a far horizon. Immediately to the north are the rocky Treshnish Islands, and Staffa, with its great cathedral caves. Farther off lie the long, low island of Tiree, which was cultivated by Columba's monks when Iona itself was no longer able to support the growing community; the mountain-island of Rum, where a hermit-monk once made his cell; the beautiful isle of Eigg, where St. Donnan, the one martyr of the early Celtic Church, met his doom at the instigation of a Pictish queen; the jagged outline of the Cuillins in Skye; and a dim speck that is Barra. Due east of Iona is the large island of Mull, with its misty mountains, its shadowy lochs, and its great deserted glens, once brimming with human life, but now the home of the red deer. To the south-east, beyond the red granite cliffs of the Ross of Mull, is the rounded outline of the Paps of Jura, with Colonsay in the foreground and Islay just beyond. Southward, some seventy miles distant and beyond the range of the eye, is the coast of Ireland. West of Iona, the vast Atlantic stretches for two thousand miles in an unbroken sweep to the shores of Labrador.

The island itself is low-lying, with numerous, irregular elevations which rarely exceed a hundred feet, though Dùn-I (pronounced Doon-ee) approaches four hundred. For its size Iona contains much variety of feature. A belt of arable land crosses the middle of the island, and a tract of it lies to the north of the Cathedral. Elsewhere, among the crags and heather, cattle and sheep find excellent pasturage. To the south lie stretches of boggy moorland, and on the heights are rocks 'that wade in heather, and upon whose brows the sea-wind waves the yellow lichen' – (Fiona Macleod). The coast-line is similarly varied: there are cliff and cave and sheltered bay, and to the north lies a great stretch of dazzling silver sand.

The landscape is treeless, though there is evidence of oak and birch in olden time and a few small trees have been reared in gardens; but there is a wonderful variety of wild flowers. The little yellow St. John's Wort (Hypericum) is reputed to have been St. Columba's favourite flower, owing perhaps to its shape, which suggests a cross. There are various land-birds, but cliff- and sea-birds predominate. These include the beautiful oyster-catcher, named in Gaelic *gille-brigde*, the servant of Bride. Seals, those soft-eyed creatures which, according to Gaelic tradition, are human beings under a spell, come sometimes to meditate on the lonelier beaches. There are no vipers on the island, though they are plentiful just across the sound in Mull. Tradition credits Columba with the immunity of the island in this respect, but a more modern explanation is the quality of the soil.

The permanent population of the island is a little fewer than a hundred, although summer residents treble that number. A hundred and fifty years ago there were no fewer than 500 souls on Iona, and they were self-sufficient except for salt. Tilling the soil, which is sweet and good in the centre of the island, still accounts for much of the permanent residents' income, and there is still useful fishing. But the days of the humming spinning-wheel by every winter fireside, the whole process – from the shearing of the sheep, the dyeing with roots and seaweeds, the carding, the spinning, to the weaving on handlooms – being carried out by the island craftsfolk for islanders' use – have long since gone.

Yet it is said that when the islands are tempest-ridden, and the mountains of Mull are cloaked in gloom, on Iona itself there is always a brightness. On a clear summer day, and particularly when the wind is in the north the beauty is idyllic. Soft cirrous clouds veil the blue vault of heaven. Over the wide, white sands the sea glistens green as an emerald; farther out it is of vivid blue, barred with purple. The granite cliffs of Mull glow rosy across the Sound, and the great mountains beyond cast their deep-blue shadow over the still waters. There is a wealth of colour, not gorgeous, but exquisite, appealing less to the senses than to the spirit, and creating a sense of peace that is balm to the world-weary. The pilgrim, the antiquarian, the artist: Iona casts her spell on all.

A note on the geology of Iona, which is remarkable. The island is immeasurably older, not only than the surrounding islands, but also than the highest mountains and most of the dry land on the earth. During the great earth-changes of the Tertiary period, the face of the globe attained, with minor differences, its present configuration. But 'the beginning of Iona is almost part of the beginning of the world itself. When our planet, from a flaming mass of combustion like the sun, shrivelled into a globe with a solid crust, and the first oceans condensed in the hollows of its surface – then it was that the Archaean rocks of which Iona and the Outer Hebrides consist were formed on the sea bottom. They contain no fossils; for, so far as is known, no living creature as yet existed in the desolate waste of waters, or on the primeval land. They were hard, rugged, and twisted; and in Iona, as elsewhere, marble has been developed by the vast heat and pressure they have undergone . . . The great Ice Age has also left its mark, for the glaciers from the hills of Mull reached out over the Sound, and, as they melted, boulders of red granite, scraped from the Ross, dropped out of the ice along the eastern shore of Iona, where they still lie, both large and small.' – (Trenholme: *Story of Iona*)

The origin of the name is a Primitive Irish word *Iwowa*, apparently

A detail of the Abbey's architecture, masonry which has to withstand the rigours of Atlantic winds.

*N*orth Iona, a
peaceful expanse of
the white sands for which
the island is famed.

*I*ona Abbey, today one
of the main features of
the miniature island which
has fascinated so many
visitors over the centuries.

derived from the word *iwos*, meaning a yew tree. Adamnan, the ninth abbot, writing in Latin at the end of the seventh century, called it Ioua insula, meaning something like 'yewy island'. Other old spellings include Eo, Ea, Io, Ia, I (pronounced 'ee'), Y, Hy, Hi and Hii (the style used by the great Northumbrian scholar Bede in the eighth century). Owing to the island's close association with Columba, the saint's name was often linked with it as, in modern Gaelic, I Chaluim Chille ('Iona of Columba of the Church'), anglicised as Icolmkill.

It is worthy of note that the Hebrew word *Iona* corresponds to the Latin *Columba*, meaning 'dove'.

Chapter Two

SCOTLAND BEFORE COLUMBA

All that we know about the religion of the pre-Christian Celts comes either from hostile sources – Greek and Latin writers at first, and Christian observers afterwards – or the impassive discoveries of antiquarian and archaeologist. The old culture went down, and its records, if there were any, have not survived. We have plenty of records of surviving pagan superstitions which may once have been part of the creed of the ancient priesthood of the Druids, who ministered to the pre-Christian Celts. St. Patrick, St. Columba and other Celtic saints have left little or nothing to tell of the faith which it was their mission to supersede. Latin and Greek commentators emphasised the elements that were quaint and barbaric, with much exaggeration.

Some Latin writers, when the Celtic provinces had been brought into the Roman Empire, tried to identify Celtic gods with members of the classical Pantheon of the 374 Celtic gods' names known from inscriptions, 305 are known only from one and only four or five of the rest occur more than twenty times. Ceasar tells us that the Druids played a leading part in public life, instructed great numbers of young men in their mysteries – esoteric, unwritten and passed on by word of mouth – and that Britain was the centre of the Druidic cult even before Gaul was conquered by Rome. Archaeology has identified ritual wells or pits in which votive offerings were thrown, including severed heads, fire ceremonies marking Beltane (May Day) and rituals with oak and mistletoe at Hallow-E'en continued in folkways long after the religion had succumbed.

There was probably much that was beautiful in the old religion, but in its later period it appears to have become degraded into a religion of witchcraft. 'It was a vague dread of innumerable spirits; the world of nature was quivering with life; in every spring and well there was a spirit; in every loch there lived some dreaded being. When the echoes of thunder rolled through the mountain corries, or when the wild storm beat the forests of oak, voices from the great Mystery were speaking.' The Druids of

A view at the North
end of Iona, Staffa,
Fingal's Cave and Mull
are visible in the
background.

*T*he west coast of Iona
which faces out
towards the Atlantic, an
ocean stretching for two
thousand miles to the
shores of Labrador.

*A*wintry aspect – the climate at this time of year is relatively mild and the snow seen here is on the hills of Mull.

*A*croft on the island of Mull, near the Ross of Mull – the glaciers of the Ice Age reached over the Sound to Iona and deposited boulders of red granite from the Ross as they melted.

Columba's time were an official class of diviners and sorcerers who professed to have powers over this spirit world, and to be able to direct the wind and weather and avert the enmity of evil spirits by means of charms and spells.

(There have been some curious survivals of pagan worship. In Iona, for example, down to the end of the eighteenth century, a solemn ceremony took place on the midnight preceding Maundy Thursday, when the 'great porridge' was cast into the western bay as an offering to the sea, that it might wash up enough seaweed for the second spring ploughing.)

Yet in spite of the darkness that prevailed at the time of Columba's coming, the task of Christian missionaries in Druidical countries was far less arduous than in some others. One suggested reason is precisely that where personal or representative gods were worshipped, existing pagan cults were more definitely organised and resistant. In this respect the Druids were as loosely bound together as, say, witch doctors; the cult of the local well or grove more significant than a generalised theocracy. The contest between the Druids and the emissaries of Christianity was keen, but it was singularly free from fanaticism and violence, and we have no record of martyrdoms such as those which characterise the later history of the Christian Church.

There is another consideration. The Christian mission from such a centre as Iona was by men of God alone, unarmed, carrying no threat in this world and offering high promise for the next. They were certainly brave men, but not in the fashion of warriors. It must be significant that the bloodthirsty Viking raids on Iona two centuries after Columba's death came at a time when kinsfolk of the Northmen were falling before the Christian armies of Charlemagne.

Columba found in the land of his adoption 'a people with a love of the arts and a passion for music, a people steeped in that mysticism, that dominating sense of the unseen without which religion is mere ignorant superstition, with that conviction of the close environment of the spiritual world that still characterises their descendents to a greater or less degree ... It needed but the trump of Christianity and the colleges became monasteries, the wells and sacred haunts were dedicated to the saints ... the revered oak tree associated with Our Lady.' – (Wilkie)

Although Iona became 'the lamp of Christ whose flame lighted pagan Europe', other lights, though mostly dim and obscure (at least so far as modern records go) had previously glimmered in these islands. The Roman Empire was officially pagan for three centuries after Christ, but the

Roman world was penetrated by a number of transcendental religions or cults. At least one of them, the Mithraic cult from Persia, was comparable and sometimes greater in its scope for long periods, as the famous temple found in the City of London after the bombing of the Second World War clearly shows. Although Christianity was a universal creed, intermittent persecution until the final proclamation of tolerance in 313 made it expedient to operate, if not in secret, at least with discretion; but, where Roman armies and Roman traders went, religions went as well, even without official backing.

There is strong reason to believe that the sturdiest growth of Christianity in Britain and Ireland was transplanted directly from the eastern Mediterranean, perhaps along trade routes to Spain or southern Gaul and northward by sea, bypassing the Roman province of Britain. The monastic organisation of the Celtic Church and other cultural conventions (for example, the psalm-singing still surviving in the Hebrides) were closer to those of the Middle East than those of the centre of empire. By the time that Christianity had become the official imperial religion, late in the fourth century, the first recorded evangelists were already at work in what is now Scotland. In the territories that had never come under imperial administration the Roman form of Church government was no more successful than the Roman secular rule. We know very little about the early forerunners of Columba and Augustine, spreading the faith without the support, and sometimes against the will, of the worldly authorities, but we can be sure they were not directly subject to Roman discipline.

St. Ninian (born *circa* 350) laboured among the southern Picts in Galloway. After Ninian came St. Patrick (born, as most scholars now agree, at Dunbriton or Dumbarton), who brought Christianity to Ireland, and established there a great school of piety and learning which was destined to produce Columba. Other saints were meanwhile at work in Scotland, but their influence was local and temporary. Even Ninian's converts became demoralised, and the country as a whole remained wrapt in pagan gloom.[1]

Of one of these early missionaries, St. Mochta, it is related that he laboured long and fruitlessly in North Britain, and returned at last to Ireland. Here his labours were crowned with success, which, however, did not obliterate the memory of his earlier defeat. It was observed that the saint, discarding the custom of his time to pray towards the east, prayed always towards the north, and he was asked the reason. He replied that at the end of a hundred years out of the north would come a dove.

The coming of Columba was predicted also by St. Patrick and St. Bride.

When Columba was born, though the barbarian tribes had descended on Rome, the Empire still stood. Justinian was emperor; Benedict had established his order at Monte Cassino; Gregory was a law student at Rome; Mahomet was not yet born. Europe was in a state of violent upheaval, and the great nations of today had not yet emerged. The Saxon tribes were invading and paganising the land that is now England, and driving the British tribes westward to the mountains. Ireland, standing apart, escaped the general devastation and became an asylum of learning.

What is now Scotland was divided into several small principalities: North and South of the Grampians were the Northern and Southern Picts; in the south-west were the Britons of Strathclyde and the Picts of Galloway; in the south-east were a group of English settlers (Angles), probably the only non-Celtic race in Scotland, whose king fortified the rock of Dunedin around which grew the city with the anglicised name of Edinburgh; and, lastly, there was a colony of Scots, or Gaelic Celts, who had crossed from Ireland in the fifth century and spread over what is now Argyll (land of the Gael) and the adjacent isles. These Scots, to which race Columba belonged, were Christian, and were destined to give to the land of their adoption its name, its royal house, and its religion.

At this period the Celtic name of Scotland was Alban, and the Latin name Scotia was applied only to Ireland, called also Hibernia.

[1] Recent researches reveal that Ninian accomplished much more than has hitherto been credited to him, his foundations having been traced all over the south and east of Scotland and as far north as Caithness. Broadly speaking, Ninian may be regarded as the apostle of the Picts and Columba as the apostle of the Scots, their main spheres of labour lying respectively east and west of Drumalbain (the ridge that traverses the Scottish Highlands from north to south). Ninian, in short, can no longer be dismissed as a mere forerunner of Columba, but shares with him the glory of Christianizing Scotland, Columba's great achievement being to complement and consolidate the work of the earlier saint.

Chapter Three

COLUMBA
IN IRELAND

Of the lives of Ninian, Bride, and Patrick, and even of Columba's contemporary, St. Mungo, we have scanty knowledge, but of Columba's achievements a remarkably clear record exists. Adamnan's *Life of St. Columba* is one of the treasures of history, and 'the most complete piece of such biography that Europe can boast of, not only at so early a period, but even through the whole Middle Ages.' – (Pinkerton: *Lives of Scottish Saints.*) It was written in Iona by Adamnan, the ninth Abbot, at the urgent request, as he tells us, of the brethren. The biographer was born in 624, twenty-seven years after the death of the saint. He conversed with men who had been Columba's monks, had access to all the literary remains, and embodied in his book the fragmentary record of an earlier Abbot. The book is in part hagiology rather than biography, and the reader must make what allowances his training and temperament demand for the prophetic and miraculous elements in the narrative.

Columba was born on 4th December, 521, at Gartan, a wild, mountainous district in Donegal, the haunt of the wolf, and of the eagle. He was descended from the royal house of Neill, his father, Phelim MacFergus, being a great-grandson of Niall of the Nine Hostings, High King of Ireland at Royal Tara from 379 to 405. In Niall's day, Ireland was a pagan land, but a certain British lad, named Patrick, was a slave in Connaught. Patrick escaped to Gaul, and in the course of time returned to Ireland, which he converted from Druidism to Christianity, and of which he became later the patron saint. Niall's son, Conall, Columba's great-grandfather, was baptised by St. Patrick.

Columba's mother, Eithne, was also of royal descent. The old Irish life of the saint says that he was eligible for the throne of Erin, which would have been offered him had he not abandoned it for the service of Christ.

There is a legend that, before her son was born, Eithne dreamed one

St. Columba portrayed in an early mediaeval manuscript.

night that an angel stood before her and offered her a robe of exquisite beauty. Scarcely was it hers than the angel took it from her and spread it out till it covered mountain and lough and forest, reaching even to Scotland. From this sign Eithne knew that her child was the child of the prophecies, and destined to lead innumerable souls to Heaven.

Columba's education was accordingly directed to fit him for his mission. He received two names: Crimthan, a wolf, and Colum, a dove, each of which seems appropriate to one element of his complex character. His early education was entrusted to Cruithnechan, an aged presbyter, renowned for sanctity, who lived near by. The child's love for the offices of the church was so marked that the children of the neighbourhood, whom he would join on coming from the cell in which he read his psalms, named him Columcille, Colum of the cell or church. Columba is, of course, the Latin form of Colum.

When his fosterage under Cruithnechan was ended, Columba was placed under the care of Finnian at an ecclesiastical school in Moville, where he was ordained deacon. Thence he proceeded to Leinster, where he studied the native literature under Gemman, the venerable Bard of that province. According to Irish tradition, he retained throughout his life the love he there acquired for the old, poetic tales of his race; and himself a poet, he probably became a member of the Order of Bards. From Master Gemman, he went on to the monastic school of St. Finnian – the most famous school in Ireland – situated by the waters of the Boyne. Finally, after a period at the monastery of Glasnevin, near Dublin, where he probably pronounced his monastic vow, he returned to his native Ulster.

In 545, Columba founded the monastery of Derry on a site given him by his kinsmen of the Clan Neill. He came to realise, however, that monasticism did not fully satisfy the needs of the time. Refreshed with a period of prayer and fasting – a visit, too, to Tours in Gaul, took place about this time – he left Derry, and began to preach up and down Ireland, attacking paganism where it still existed, and strengthening the faith in other parts. Everywhere he founded churches, of which over three hundred are ascribed to him; and monasteries, of which the most famous are Durrow and Kells. The power of organisation was one of his many gifts, and Scotland reaped the fruits of his Irish experience. His method was to find a suitable site where a church was needed, and go boldly to the owner and ask for it; then, when permission was given, he erected the requisite buildings – not scrupling to work with his own hands when necessary – installed carefully trained workers and passed on; and, in spite of his constant journeyings, he continued to keep in touch with all his foundations.

Why Columba left Ireland for Scotland is not known with certainty. A popular account has it that the saint, who was a fervent scribe and highly skilled in the art of illumination, secretly copied for his own use a beautiful manuscript of the book of Psalms, belonging to his old master, Finnian of Moville. The owner demanded the copy, which was refused. Finnian appealed to Diarmaid, King of Ireland, and chief of the southern Clan Neill. The king gave judgment in these words: 'To every cow belongs her calf, and to every book its copy.' Columba, filled with wrath at the decision, incited his kinsmen of the northern Clan Niall to battle, and Diarmaid was defeated with great slaughter. Columba was then summoned by Diarmaid before a synod and excommunicated; but the sentence was afterwards annulled. Full of remorse for his deed, Columba sought his 'anmcara', his soulfriend or spiritual adviser, who counselled him that, as a penance, he should go into perpetual exile, and win as many souls for Christ as he had caused bodies to be slain in battle.

This narrative is not reliable. Adamnan not only does not mention it, but he speaks of Columba's having revisited Ireland on ten different occasions. It is more likely that his departure from Ireland was concerned with the position of his kinsfolk in the Scottish Dalriada (Argyllshire), so named after the Irish Dalriada (Antrim), whence they came. (The channel which separates the two countries is only twelve miles wide, and the houses in Kintyre can be seen from the Irish coast opposite). The northern Picts were at this time a barbarous and pagan race; the southern Britons had lapsed sadly since the days of Ninian; and the Scots were the only Christian people in North Britain. In 560 the Scots settlers suffered a crushing defeat at the hands of Brude, King of the Northern Picts; their king, a kinsman of Columba, was slain; and there was a danger that the whole colony might be extirpated. In Skene's opinion (and in accordance with a prophecy in the Chronicle of the Picts and Scots) it was this reverse which called forth the mission of St. Columba, and led him to select North Pictland as his first field. Christianity was to be the bond which should unite these turbulent nations, and establish among them an abiding peace.

Adamnan puts the reason for Columba's departure quite simply: 'In the forty-second year of his age, desiring to seek a foreign country for the sake of Christ, he sailed from Ireland to Britain.'

The west coast of the island — until the end of the eighteenth century 'great porridge' was cast into the western bay as an offering on the midnight preceding Maunday Thursday to assure the supply of seaweed for the second spring ploughing.

Alba Pictures

Cairns at the bay where St. Columba landed, they are believed to have been built by mediaeval monks and pilgrims.

Chapter Four

IONA

In 563, Columba, accompanied by twelve followers, sailed from Derry in a frail coracle of wicker and hides. After visiting his kinsmen in the Scottish Dalriada, he continued his journey northwards. According to tradition, he landed first on Oronsay, but, on discovering that his fatherland was still in sight, he re-embarked, and set his prow for Iona. On the hill a little westward of Port à Churaich, the Bay of the Coracle, where Columba landed, is a small cairn, called Carn Cul ri Eirinn, the Cairn of-the-back-to-Erin. Here, it is said, Columba scanned the southern horizon, and, satisfied that his beloved land was out of sight, buried the coracle on the beach, and entered into possession.

Iona was, in most respects, admirably suited for Columba's purpose. Its position on the line which divided the Christian Scots of Argyll from the pagan Picts made it a convenient strategic centre for mission work. It had also natural advantages, as the eighth Duke of Argyll points out in his little book, *Iona*. 'On the eastern side was the channel which he had missed, giving much-needed shelter from prevailing winds. Above all, it was a fertile island, giving promise of ample sustenance for man and beast. It is true Iona is a rocky island, the bones protruding at frequent intervals through the skin of turf. Even there, however, Columba must have seen that the pasture was close and good, and not far from the spot on which he first swept the southern sky he must have found that the heathy and rocky hills subsided into a lower tract, green with that delicious turf which, full of thyme and wild clover, gathers upon soils of shelly sand. This tract is called in Gaelic the 'Machair' or Sandy Plain. A little farther on he must soon have found that the eastern or sheltered side presented a slope of fertile soil exactly suiting the essential conditions of ancient husbandry – a tract of land which was as admirably adapted for the growth of corn as the remainder of it was suited to the support of flocks and herds.'

According to the Irish annals, the island was granted to Columba by Conall, the sixth king of the Scottish Dalriada; according to the vulnerable Bede, it was granted by Brude, King of the Northern Picts. 'The probability is,' says Huyshe, 'that Columba found Iona unoccupied and unclaimed, that Conall promised not to disturb his occupation of it, and

Alba Pictures

Carn Cul Ri Eirinn (Cairn of the Back to Ireland) which marks a spot frequented by St. Columba during his lifetime.

that, when the Picts were converted to Christianity by Columba, King Brude sanctioned his right and title to the little island.'

Of the buildings erected by Columba little trace remains, and what there is requires scholarly interpretation. The vallum, or boundary wall, of the early Christian period has been clearly plotted, excavation has determined the sites of various pits and post holes, and the base of the tiny chapel beside the west door of the Abbey church, now restored and called 'St. Columba's Shrine' is pre-mediaeval. The positioning of the high crosses immediately to the west and inconclusive descriptions of walls uncovered during the restoration of the nave eighty years ago suggest that the site of the Columban church and a conjectural later stone church may have been there.

However, in Columba's day stone was not used when there was plenty of wood, either for crosses or for buildings. Some dozens of early Christian carved stones have been found, but none that seems likely to have been designed for a wall. The original buildings were constructed on the Irish model, and were probably a mere collection of huts composed of timber and wattle, surrounded by a vallum of earth. We can picture it fairly clearly from Adamnan's references: the oaken church with the sacristy adjoining it; the refectory with its fire-place and its stone vessel of water where the feet of tired pilgrims were washed, the kitchen near by; the guest chamber; the mill, the barn, the stable; the individual huts of the monks arranged round the enclosures; and, apart, the hut of the Abbot.

'The glory of these buildings was within,' says Riley. 'It is by no means impossible,' he goes on, 'that the severe simplicity, as well as the uniformity of plan and size, which usually characterise our early churches, was less the result of the poverty or ignorance of their founders than of choice, originating in the spirit of their faith, or veneration for some model given them by their first teachers; for that the earliest Christian churches on the continent before the time of Constantine were like these, small and unadorned, there is no reason to doubt.'

The rule of the monastery in Iona, as in Ireland, enforced strict observance of religious duty, and ascetic practice. Obedience, Celibacy, Poverty, Caution and Reason in Speech, and Humility, these were its main features; and specially characteristic of Iona, Hospitality and Kindness to Animals. The monks called their Abbot Father; to him they were children, to one another brethren, and from the earliest times the community is spoken of as the Family of Hy.

The first two years of Columba's residence in Iona were spent in learning the language, tilling the soil, training followers, and generally in organising the community. The days were filled with prayer, study, and manual labour, and in this last Columba, with his great spiritual and intellectual gifts, was always ready to share. 'In dairy, granary, or in the fields, each worshipped God in his appointed task, and made his toil a sacramental thing.' – (Troup.)

But these men were not recluses, and monastic routine did not satisfy them. The Columban Church was a missionary church, and its founder was preparing his followers for the great enterprise of converting an entirely pagan land to Christianity. His plan was to begin by attacking Pictish paganism in its stronghold, at the court of Brude at Inverness, and when the time was ripe he set forth with two carefully chosen comrades, St. Kenneth and St. Comgall, both Irish Picts, who knew the language of Brude's court.

The route lay due north-east, through the Great Glen of Alba, with its continuous line of long, narrow lochs, now linked by the Caledonian Canal. So wild a region, with its dark, brooding mountains and primeval forests, could be traversed only on foot, and the whole adventure must have involved the 'perils of water, perils of robbers, perils by the heathen, perils in the wilderness,' known to the Apostles of old. They reached their destination without hurt, but Brude, encouraged by Briochan, the chief Druid, refused them admittance. At the sign of the Cross, however – so the legend has it – the bolted gates flew open, and the awestruck king capitulated. Be that as it may, it is certain that Brude was won by the message of Columba, and embraced the Christian religion. Thus did the powerful King of Picts, the race which had withstood the legions of Rome herself, succumb to three soldiers of Christ.

To have converted the Pictish king was nominally to have converted the Pictish people, but Columba's aim was to establish a living faith throughout the land. Bands of trained workers came on from Iona, and there ensued years of untiring labour during which Brude remained a staunch friend. By precept and example the Picts were gradually won over; churches were built; and in every valley Columba placed some 'sentry for Christ.'

The political effects of Columba's mission are not to be ignored. His royal descent and his kinship with the noblest familes of Ireland and the Scottish Dalriada would alone have made him a power politically; but, apart from this, the first ten years of his labours in Scotland established him as a statesman no less than as a religious leader of uncommon gifts. In winning the Picts to Christianity he had secured peace between the tribes, and prepared the way for political union. His reputation for wisdom and saintliness was now such that he was frequently called upon to settle disputes between the clans; the King of Strathclyde sent to consult him regarding his future; and when the King of the Scottish Dalriada died, it was Columba who appointed his successor, Aidan, who went to Iona for consecration at the saint's hands. (This is the earliest record of a royal coronation in Great Britain.) In 575, at the famous Convention of Drumceatt in Ireland, Columba accomplished three objects of note: first, the 'staying' of the Bards, whose sentence of explusion because of their annoying exactions of hospitality, he had replaced by the imposition of restrictive rules, thus preserving a great Irish institution; secondly, the exemption of women from military service; and, thirdly, the political independence of the Scottish Dalriada, thus settling a long-standing quarrel between the Irish king and the King of Argyll.

This tract of land is called the Machair in gaelic which is formed from grassland on dunes.

Alba Pictures

Columba has been accredited with martial propensities, and according to tradition was concerned in more than one battle fought on Irish soil. Dr. Reeves, commenting on this, says we must bear in mind the complexion of the times and the peculiar condition of society, of which civil faction seemed almost part and parcel.

When the Northern and Southern Picts were united, Columba sent his missionaries southwards as far as the Forth and the Clyde. South of this another saint was at work: Kentigern – better known as Mungo, the Beloved One – far-famed for the austere simplicity of his life. The saint had been trained at the school of St. Serf in Fife, and had made his centre at Cathures, now Glasgow. In one of his missionary journeys Columba is said to have satisfied a long-felt desire to visit his unknown brother. 'When Mungo heard that the Apostle of the North was near at hand, he marshalled his little company; the children led the way, followed by the novices, then the older monks, and the the holy man himself.... As the two processions drew near, one company chanted the portion of a psalm, and from the others in the distance came the response.' – (Troup.) After enjoying Mungo's frugal hospitality for many days, Columba departed, the saints having exchanged pastoral staves in token of their mutual love of Christ.

*S*t. Oran's Chapel, standing near the Abbey, with the Reilig Odhrain or Graveyard of the Kings.

Alba Pictures

The places visited and churches founded in Columba's lifetime all over the mainland and the isles are numerous. Daughter monasteries arose, but Iona remained the 'citadel and retreat' of the Celtic missionaries.

The monks must have been skilled and daring navigators. Adamnan mentions several types of boats belonging to the island fleet: the coracle of wicker and hide, the bark, the skiff, the coble, the freight-ship, and the long boat hollowed out of a single oak or pine tree. The most famous of the sailor-monks was Cormac, who penetrated to Orkney and Shetland, and, it is thought probable, to the Faröes and Iceland. Columba himself, like all Celts, loved the sea, and long after his death was invoked by sailors in storm. 'He who is wise with the wisdom of a hundred storms,' says Kenneth Macleod, 'will have two tillers to his rudder: the Art of the Druids for the luck of Wind, and the Faith of Iona for the Stilling of the Waves.'

It is not known how long before his death Columba ceased travelling. From work he never ceased, and in later years he probably gave much of his time to the copying of manuscripts, and art in which he was highly skilled. Two splendid manuscripts are commonly attributed to him – the *Cathach*, a Psalter (in the Library of the Royal Irish Academy), and the *Book of Durrow*, the Gospels (in the Library of Trinity College, Dublin). He was not only a scribe but a poet, and probably a member of the Order of Bards which he defended at Drumceatt. Of the large poetical output attributed to him, three fine Latin hymns and several poems in his native Gaelic are preserved.

Stories of Columba's visionary powers abound in Adamnan's pages. In our modern civilisation, what is called 'second sight' is generally regarded as mere superstition; yet even amongst the classes we call educated, and especially in our 'Celtic fringes,' there are not a few who believe it to be 'a quickened inward vision,' a veritable sixth sense, as real as the physical senses, or more so. 'The faculty itself is so apt to the spiritual law,' says Fiona Macleod, 'that one wonders why it is so set apart in doubt.' To one who marvelled at his power, Columba made reply: 'Heaven has granted to some to see on occasion in their mind, clearly and surely, the whole of earth and sea and sky.'

Adamnan records of Columba that 'he could not pass the space even of a single hour without applying himself either to prayer, or reading, or writing, or else to some manual labour.' He tells us how children loved him – one climbed to his knee in a poor man's house – and how the saint loved animals – he sent a monk to tend a storm-tossed crane alighted from Ireland, till after three days it was ready to fly forth. When Columba was more or less tied by frailty to the island – save for his retreats to Hinba, an unidentified islet where a monastery for recluses and penitents existed, and where Eithne, the saint's mother, is said to be interred – many came from far distances to seek help and counsel. Pilgrims of all degrees were constantly ferried across the strait from Mull by the monks of Iona. To the end Columba was lord and servant of all.

In the month of May, in the seventy-seventh year of his life, Columba, too feeble to walk the distance between the monastery and the field where the monks were at work, was carried over to the Machair in a cart, and here he told the sorrowing brethren that his end was at hand. On a Saturday in early June, he set forth with his faithful servant Diormit, and took leave of the old familiar places. In the granary he blessed the store of grain, and as he returned to the monastery he rested halfway, at a spot where a cross was afterwards placed. Here, Adamnan tells us, the old white horse that used to carry the milk-pails between the byre and the monastery came up and put its head in the Abbot's lap, whinnying and shedding copious tears; and when Diormit tried to drive him away, Columba stayed his attendant's hand, and 'blessed his sorrowing servant the horse.'

He then ascended the little hill overlooking the monastery, and blessed the island, uttering the prophetic words quoted in the introduction of this book. Returning to his cell, he sat transcribing the Psalter, but when he got as far as verse 10 of Psalm xxxiv: 'They that seek the Lord shall not want any good things,' he stopped, saying: 'Let Baithen finish it.' Resting on his bed after vespers that evening, he gave Diormit a message to the brethren: 'This, dear children, is my last message to you – that you preserve with each other sincere charity and peace.'

When the midnight bell tolled for nocturns, he rose with a last effort, and made his way to the church. Diormit, full of dread, followed his master, calling: 'Where art thou, Father?' Groping his way in the darkness, he found the saint lying before the altar, and laid the holy head on his lap. The monks came running with lights, and at the sight of their dying master fell a-weeping. His face lit with joy, the saint made a feeble movement of benediction, 'and immediately breathed forth his spirit.'

After three days of vigil, his remains were interred in a simple grave, in the manner of the time.

IONA – A HISTORY OF THE ISLAND

*T*he beautiful white sands of the sacred island from which the monks set sail in a variety of boats; the coracle, of wicker and hide, the bark, the shiff, the cobble, the long boat and the freight-ship are all mentioned by a former abbot.

Dennis Hardley

Chapter Five
THE
CELTIC CHURCH

The Lamp that Lighted Pagan Europe

The Celtic Church established by Columba in Scotland in the sixth century endured until the death of Malcolm Canmore in the eleventh, when it gave place to the church of Rome; and even after the religious revolution of that period, the Culdees, a body of Celtic ecclesiastics, can be traced down to the fourteenth century.

The Venerable Bede, a contemporary of Adamnan, tells us that Columba 'left successors distinguished for their great charity, divine love, and strict attention to discipline.' For many generations, indeed, that marching soul led men to great enterprises and successful issues. From Scotland, the Iona missionaries passed to England and the continent of Europe. They it was, along with their brothers from Ireland, who brought Christianity to the greater part of Germany and Switzerland, and even to part of Italy; and their names are known from Iceland to Tarentum. The Convent of Erfurt, which produced Luther, is believed to have been a Celtic foundation, the last to survive in Germany; and at Milan, at St. Gall in Switzerland, and at Wurzburg, there may be seen manuscripts executed by men who had learned penmanship and theology in Iona or her daughter monasteries. The little island became supreme not only over the numerous monasteries created by her sons, but also over the senior foundations in Ireland. In the seventh century, she was at the height of her fame: the centre of a vast area of missionary activity, a renowned theological school, and a seat of learning.

Martyrdoms are all but unknown in the early history of the Celtic Church, and its saints are therefore not martyrs, but founders of churches and great teachers whose work and spirit survived and inspired those who came after them. Their names linger in many parts of Scotland. Loch Columcille in Skye, and the Isle of Inchcolm (Colum's Isle) in the Firth of Forth commemorate two of the many monasteries founded by Columba himself. The Cathedral of Aberdeen is dedicated to St. Machar, a successor of Drostan, who, along with Columba, converted a Pictish fort at Deer into a monastery, the centre of missionary work in East Pictland. The name of the martyr Donnan survives in Kildonan, of Blane of Bute in

Dunblane, of Mun in Kinmun, of Finnan in Glenfinnan, of Maelrubha in Loch Maree. Up and down the western seaboard and throughout the isles are scattered the remains of little Celtic chapels and monastic cells, built by these holy men.

Comparatively little is known about the system and theology of the Celtic Church and the whole subject has given rise to much controversy. Presbyterian, Episcopalian, and Roman Catholic alike have claimed for their particular communion affinity in doctrine or usage with the Church of Columba. 'The striking fact,' says Troup, 'is that they meet round his memory.' But while all modern religious bodies may claim a share in the spiritual inheritance of the ancient Church, it is certain that none resembles it outwardly.

The Celtic Church was monastic in form. Monasticism was probably first established within the Christian Church by St. Basil, in the East. In the fourth century, St. Jerome introduced it into Western Europe, and St. Martin of Tours into Gaul. Thence it was brought by St. Ninian to Strathclyde, and a little later by St. Patrick to Ireland. It was the modified Irish form of monasticism – less formalistic, and more vigorous and bracing than that of the East – that Columba established in Iona. Its monasteries were not destined for recluses – though the church had its anchorites – but were rather religious settlements where men were fitted to go out into the world, and preach and minister to all and sundry. 'The secret of the early Celts lay in this, that they linked sacrament with service, altar with hearth, worship with work.' – (Troup.) Their active and enterprising spirit succeeded in creating the great missionary church that the times demanded.

Columba constituted his church on the model of the family, and the source of jurisdiction was vested in the Abbot. For over two hundred years after the Founder's death, the Abbot was chosen from his kin, in accordance with Irish tradition and clan feeling. In later days, when the clergy commonly married, hereditary succession was common also in benefices.

Diocesan episcopacy was unknown, but there were bishops of a sort. They appear to have been a very numerous body, appointed for the purpose of ordaining deacons and priests in their respective monasteries. In other respects, we gather, they lived the same life as the rest of the community, though honour was shown to the office.

Ordinations seem to have been irregular, personal qualifications being deemed more essential than ceremony. 'More Scotico,' indeed, was used as a term of reproach amongst the Roman Catholic clergy, who exalted organisation. 'The Christian virtues of humility and meekness,' says Miss Bentinck Smith, 'in which the emissaries of the British Church found Augustine deficient, were valued in Iona above orthodoxy and correctness of religious observance.'

'It was a marked and distinctive feature of the Iona system that while missionary monks, North and South, willingly yielded corporate obedience to Iona, and loyally owned Columba's authority, they were always allowed individual liberty and freedom of judgment.' – (Troup.) In later days, when great spiritual leaders were lacking, this freedom tended to degenerate into licence, and the loose organisation of the Church led eventually, as we shall see, to her corporate decay.

The precise nature of the doctrines of the Celtic Church is not clearly known, but from scattered allusions we gather that the scriptures were the basis of teaching.

The monks appear to have enjoyed a very liberal education. They were all bi-lingual in Latin and Gaelic, and probably many were, like Adamnan, proficient in Hebrew and Greek as well. Within the monasteries, the services were conducted in the Latin tongue, but the monks preached to the people in their native Gaelic.

Not a few of the monks, in successive generations, were distinguished in poetry, rhetoric, general philosophy, and science (including astronomy). A love of the useful and fine arts was inculcated, and so highly was music valued that in the early days the faculty was regarded as a gift bestowed by heaven only on its favourites.

The work of the Celtic Church, south of the Border, is specially worthy of notice, for the evangelisation of England is so generally accredited to St. Augustine – as in large measure it ought to be – that the share of Iona in the task is too apt to be overlooked.

St. Augustine landed in Kent shortly after Columba's death. One of his companions, Paulinus by name, went to Northumbria and made many converts, including King Edwin. Edwin, however, was slain in battle, and the new faith was discarded. Oswald, the heir to the throne, took refuge in Scotland, and received part of his education in Iona.

On regaining his kingdom, his first care was to re-establish the Christian Church, and it was to Iona, not to Canterbury, that he turned for help. Aidan was sent, in 635, and he built a monastery, after the Iona pattern, on the little island of Lindisfarne (Holy Island), off the east coast of Northumbria. He preached to the people, at first, in his native Gaelic, while the king sat at his feet, interpreting. Numbers of Scots missionaries followed Aidan, and Lindisfarne became a centre of missionary enterprise second only to Iona.

Aidan's successors, St. Finan and St. Colman, added fresh lustre to the southern monastery. Whitby, later the home of Caedmon, was one of her daughter houses; and so, too, was Melrose, which in turn produced St. Cuthbert, the apostle of the Lothians, whose name is borne by a famous church in Edinburgh.

St. Aidan and his followers not only restored to Christianity areas that had lapsed since the invasion of the Germanic tribes from which our island race is mainly descended, but also succeeded in winning over districts which their predecessors had not been able to enter. From the Celtic missionaries in the north and from the Roman missionaries in the south, there flowed two streams of missionary work that eventually covered the whole land. 'The simplicity, the devotion, the free spirit, the tenderness and love, the apostolic zeal of the missionaries of Iona combined with the more complete organisation and the higher culture of which Rome was the schoolmistress, (was) to form the English Church.' – (Bishop Lightfoot of Durham.)

In some respects Celtic missionaries, and the missionaries they trained, were more successful than the missionaries from Rome, who

A view towards St. Mary's church and priory on Lindisfarne, the Holy Island, off the east coast of Northumbria.

Dennis Hardley

tended to be diplomats and politicians first and evangelists second. The preachers from the north were more direct, more fervent and more populist. An example was St. Cedd who, Bede tells us, was eldest of four brothers trained for the church by Aidan at Holy Island. When the East Saxons, originally converted by Augustine's mission, reverted to paganism, Cedd was chosen as bishop to bring them back to the Church. He did this to good effect, and the succession to the Bishops of the East Saxons are probably the Bishops of London, next in precedence in the Church of England after the Archbishops of Canterbury and York.

There was more than rivalry in devotion between the two sources of mission, because there had been little day-to-day contact between Gaeldom and Rome. In 463 Rome and the Continental Churches had adopted a new method of calculating the date of Easter, but the Churches of Gaels, Britons and Picts retained the old computation, which they believed to have been derived from the East, from the Apostle John himself. In 664, King Oswy of Northumbria summoned a synod, or council, at Whitby in Yorkshire to settle these differences. Cedd, being a Saxon with Celtic training, although he personally favoured the Celtic practice, acted, Bede tells us, as a most careful interpreter for both parties.[1]

Practices differed also on the tonsure and the strictness of clerical celibacy. Bede gives a full account of the arguments the parties used. What seems to have convinced the king in the end was the appeal to the authority of Rome based on Christs admonition to St. Peter. 'Although your fathers were holy men,' the Roman advocate said, 'do you imagine that they, a few men in a corner of a remote island, are to be preferred before the universal Church of Christ throughout the world?' The king, who had hitherto favoured Celtic practice, declared for Rome. This ended the supremacy of the Celtic Church in South Britain.

The paschal question had previously estranged the Roman missionaries from the Welsh Christians, and was still to create dissension in North Britain. After Augustine reached England, Gregory wrote cautioning him against the rigorous enforcement of Roman usages, and advised him rather to choose from the customs of different churches those which seemed particularly suited to the place and the people. Augustine, however, gifted man as he was, lacked the tolerance and foresight of the great Pope, and while it is a matter of opinion whether or not he and his followers were wise in refusing to compromise in this particular issue, it is certain that they failed in dealing with the Celtic peoples, as others have since failed, because of 'that passion for complete uniformity which has so frequently worked mischief in human affairs.' – (Rait.) Sheer tenacity of opinion, however, often overcomes a plastic temperament, and Adamnan, visiting Northumbria twenty-four years after the Synod of Whitby, did not fail to be moved by the rebuke of many learned ecclesiastics, that a small and obscure community like the Family of Hy should venture to defy the wisdom and might of Rome, on so important an issue. The gentle, scholarly Abbot, who 'shared the prevailing over-estimate of these things,' returned to Iona – where, according to the old Irish chronicle, his appearance with the coronal tonsure of Rome in place of the Celtic half-shaven head was 'a great surprise to his congregation' – and dutifully pointed out to the brethern the error of their ways. The brethern, however, refused to diverge from the ancient customs, and a schism was created, which persisted long after Adamnan's death. Meanwhile the Roman party grew steadily stronger, and in 717, Naiton, King of Picts, expelled from his kingdom all monks who refused to conform. One by one, Iona gave in on all the controversial points, and by 772, unity was restored within the Celtic Church.

[1] An old Gazetteer of Scotland gives a vigorous, if somewhat biased account of this episode:–

'A celebrated, but very stupid dispute, at Whitby, in Yorkshire, between Colman, one of its alumni, and Wilfred, a Romanist, on the precious questions as to when Easter or the Passover should be celebrated, and with what kind of tonsure the hair of a professed religious should be cut, conducted on the one side by an appeal to the traditional authority of John the apostle, and on the other to the interpolated dictum of Peter, the alleged janitor of heaven, and supported on the part of Colman with all the zeal and influence of his Culdee brethren, ended, as it deserved to do, in the total discomfiture of the people of Iona, who totally forgot the moral dignity of their creed both by the jejuneness of the questions debated, and by the monstrous folly of appealing to the verdict of the Northumbrian Prince Oswi, a diademed ninny, who 'determined on no account to disregard the institutions of Peter who kept the keys of the kingdom of heaven' – this dispute gave a virtual death-blow to Culdeeism, and the influence of Icolmkill in England.... Under Adamnan, who died in 703, Iona proclaimed to the world its having commenced a career of apostasy... the ecclesiastics of the island put some trappings of finery upon their originally simple form of church government, they fraternised with the Romanists on the subject of keeping Easter... and though continuing to maintain the island's literary fame, very seriously defiled the essential purity of Christian faith and devotion.'

Chapter Six

LATER HISTORY

The first two centuries of the Columban Church were the most glorious period in the history of Iona. 'In later years,' says Rait, '(the Church) did not escape the inevitable deterioration, and it had its reformers.... After the time of Columba, it seems to have had little influence in national affairs, but the persistence of its individual life indicates that it possessed a real hold upon the people of Scotland.' Its best work was done as a missionary church; later, as civilisation advanced, and the need of the times tended towards an organised religion, it was found lacking, and inevitably went down before the disciplined forces of Rome.

Hardly were its internal troubles over when a new danger threatened the Iona community from without. A series of invasions by Danish pirates is recorded: In 797, the island was pillaged; and in 801–2, the monastery was burned to the ground; and in 806, Iona for the first time suffered red martyrdom,' in the slaughter of sixty-eight monks, traditionally at Martyr's Bay. The afflicted monastery could no longer continue the oversight of the Church, and in 814, the primacy was transferred temporarily to Kells, in Ireland. The Iona monks, however, clung to their island, and bravely proceeded to build a new monastery, of stone, and on a better site, where the Abbey Church now stands.

In 825, there was a second Danish massacre, the heathen bursting into the church one dark winter morning, during the celebration of Mass, and cutting down Blathmac, the acting superior, together with several of his monks. This is commemorated as the Passion of St. Blathmac and the Martyrs of Iona.

The primacy did not go back to Iona, but passed in Scotland to Dunkeld, where Constantine, King of Picts, had erected a monastery far from the danger zone. Thence it passed to Abernethy, and finally, in 908, to St. Andrews. In Iona the office of Abbot was succeeded by that of Coarb of Columkill (Heir of Columba), held usually by the abbot of one of the greater Irish monasteries, who ruled Iona from afar. Thenceforward Iona, like the Celtic Church generally, steadily declined in importance.

Following the turbulent ninth century, there came a long period of

Dennis Hardley

Caledonian MacBrayne's M.V. Columba in the Sound of Mull, passing the Abbey, the means of transportation has changed somewhat since Columba's day.

relative peace, and henceforth there are many blanks in the history of Iona. The Danish invaders were succeeded by the Norse Vikings, but these were not aggressive towards the monastery. (The Danes, it may be said in fairness, are believed to have been incited to animosity against the Church because of the slaughter of their pagan kinsmen in North Germany by Charlemagne in the name of Christianity.)

In 980, a notable pilgrim, Anlaf, King of the Danes of Dublin, came to Iona after his defeat by the Irish, and spent his last days there in penance and good works. (Two centuries earlier, Neill Frassach, King of Ireland, and Artgal, King of Connaught, had died in Iona, having relinquished their thrones for the monastic life.) Six year later, the Danes once more descended on the island, and slaughtered the Abbot and fifteen monks, traditionally on the White Sands.

During the rest of the Celtic Church period, the possession of the Western Isles fluctuated between Scotland and Norway. In 1098, King

Magnus of Norway (called Magnus Barelegs because of his adoption of the kilt during his long operations in the Hebrides) anchored his war-galleys in the Sound of Mull, and came ashore to do homage to the Isle of Columba.

Nothing more is heard of Iona for sixty-five years, when a notice appears in the Annals of Ulster of a deputation to Ireland in 1164.

In the meantime, important developments in the kingdom and Church of Scotland began in the reign of Malcolm Canmore and his second wife, the Saxon princess Margaret. Malcolm, after taking refuge in England, wrested the throne of Scotland from Macbeth; Margaret took refuge in Scotland after the Norman conquest of England. 'That Queen Margaret achieved a reformation in manners and morals among the Scots,' writes Professor Duncan, 'may well be questioned in ecclesiastical affairs and is without supporting evidence in secular.' She was certainly devout, and brought in the Benedictine monks to found Dunfermline Abbey, in which she and her husband were buried. She was also indifferent to the culture of her husband's people; none of their six sons was brought up to speak Gaelic and they were all given English names, a grave affront to anyone jealous of the traditions of the Gaelic royal line. The language of the court was henceforth Scottis (Scots) derived from the Anglian settlers in the Lothians. At the same time, Margaret supported and encouraged native devotion to native saints, and was little concerned with innovation in monastic life generally in Scotland.

The evidence for her distress at various abuses in the Scottish Church is slender and partial, and indeed it is only the Norman chronicler Ordericus Vitalis who tells us that she 'restored the monastery of Hy, which Columba, the servant of Christ, had erected in the time of Brude, son of Meilcon, King of Picts. It had fallen into ruin in the storms of war and the lapse of ages, but the faithful queen rebuilt and restored it, and gave the monks an endorsement for the performance of the Lord's works'.

If this is true, it left no trace on the island that archaeology can find in our day. The eldest of the three sons who succeeded to the throne, Edgar, thought so little of the Iona connection that in 1098 he accepted Norwegian sovereignty over all the islands to the west of the Scottish mainland. His brother David I abolished the Celtic liturgy, organised regular dioceses administered by bishops and parish priests, and replaced the Celtic monks and Culdees by Benedictine monks and Augustinian canons and canonesses. By the end of his reign in 1153, practically all the mediaeval sees had been founded.

St. Oran's Chapel, probably built by Somerled as a mortuary chapel for himself and his descendants, is the oldest surviving building on Iona.

The Culdees mentioned above were an order instituted in Dublin by St. Maelruain in 787. The name is derived from the Celtic *Cele De*, the servant of God. They were hermits, leading a life of prayer and contemplation, and, by the ninth century, their cells were scattered over Scotland. Later, they fell away in many places from the old strict rules, and this served as an excuse for their suppression in the reform of the Scottish Church in the twelfth century.

During the twelfth century there emerged in the Hebrides and Argyll a new Gaelic-Norse society which under Somerled ('summer voyager') seized control of the southern isles from the Norse King of Man. It was probably Somerled who built St Oran's Chapel, the oldest surviving building on Iona, as a mortuary chapel for himself and his descendants. He died in 1164, and it was his son Ranald or Reginald who founded the present mediaeval Abbey, a Benedictine house, and the Augustinian Nunnery.

From Ranald were descended the three great Gaelic families of Macdonald (who later took the title of Lords of the Isles) masters of Islay and Kintyre; Macdougall, lords of Argyll, Mull, Coll and Tiree, and the lords of Garmoran (the northern territories). They were an adventurous, piratical and thrusting people, who played off the kings of Scotland, Norway and England against one another for several centuries. Although the Western Isles were in a Norwegian diocese, Iona Abbey was given exemption from episcopal jurisdiction by the Vatican in 1203.

The Irish Annals record the building in 1204 'without any right, and in dishonour of the community' and a party of Derry men came over and pulled down the work. There is no other record of the event, a melancholy postscript to six and a half centuries of the Family of Hy. A Norwegian chronicle records a 'Viking' in 1210 when the opposed forces at the end of a protracted civil war joined in an old-fashioned expedition on which they pillaged 'the holy island, which Norwegians have always held sacred.'

There is no Hebridean record of this escapade, and in 1986 the Iona Cathedral Trust (see below) felt it could be ignored in celebrating a thousand years of peace with a special book of remembrance to record benefactors of the Abbey. Indeed, the Lords of the Isles and other Highland chiefs appear to have been generous patrons of the Abbey and of the important school of mediaeval sculpture that was established there. Only Clonmacnois in Ireland can match Iona's collection of Celtic sculpted stones in number; in quality it is unmatched. The best are now displayed, sheltered from erosion, in the cloisters, the rebuilt infirmary and the Abbey church, and the thoughtful visitor can only regret the centuries of neglect that erased the message of so many of their fellows.

The cession of the Western Isles from Norway to Scotland in 1266 still left them technically in the Norwegian archdiocese of Trondheim until 1472, but the patronage of the diocese of the Isles was transferred to the King of Scots and Iona seems to have developed a special relationship with the see of Dunkeld. Although the memorial sculpture continued to develop, the Abbey buildings went through a period of neglect followed by a major repair and extension initiated by Abbot Dominic, who succeeded in 1421. As a necessary preliminary he had to go about resuming control of the Abbey's endowments which had been farmed out and treated as private revenues by various associates of the Abbey. The two houses, Abbey and Nunnery, drew revenues from properties as far afield as North Uist and Skye in one direction and southern Kintyre in the other. Abbot Dominic complained about the encroachment on Abbey lands of 'wicked and perverse noblemen' and was forced to spend time on going to law before rebuilding could begin. Abbot John Mackinnon, who succeeded in 1467, completed the rebuilding of the Abbey and probably oversaw the elaborate tomb recess in St. Oran's Chapel for one of the last of the line of the Lordship.

In 1493 James IV finally suppressed the troublesome Lordship of the Isles and incorporated the title into his own; it is now part of the honours of the heir to the throne of the United Kingdom. In 1498, on the petition of the Earl of Argyll, the King asked the Vatican to elect the Abbacy into the Bishopric of the Isles, and by 1506 this was accomplished. For a couple of generations the liturgical and artistic work on Iona continued, even without the long established patronage of Clan Donald; but once again a strong protecting hand had gone.

In 1549, Donald Monro, Dean of the Isles, visited the island, and from him we have a picture of Iona twelve years before the Reformation, when the community was swept into exile. 'Within this ile,' he writes, 'there is a monastery of mounckes, and ane uther of nuns, with a paroche-kirke, and sundrie uther chapells, dotat of auld by the Kings of Scotland and by Clandonald of the iyles.'

Many precious manuscripts and books are said to have been carried off by the dispersed monks to the Scots monastery at Ratisbon and the

Scots colleges at Douay and Rome, but none of these has been identified.

There is no evidence that any systematic attempt to destroy the buildings was made at the time of the Reformation in 1560, when the island and the lands formerly belonging to the monastery passed into the hands of MacLean of Duart.

In 1609, Andrew Knox, who was made Bishop of the Isles in the temporary episcopate established a year later, held a convention of several chiefs of the highlands and islands, on Iona. Here the 'Statutes of Icolmkill' were drawn up and subscribed, the chiefs pledging themselves to repair the churches throughout their territories, to provide parish ministers, to promote the observance of the Sabbath day, and to endeavour to put a stop to certain undesirable practices which were then prevalent.

In 1617, the Abbey of Iona was annexed to the Bishopric of the Isles. Eighteen years later, Charles I wrote to MacLean of Duart asking him to restore the Island of Icolmkill to the Bishop, and in the same year ordered the Lords of the Exchequer to pay to the Bishop the sum of £400 for the restoration of the Abbey Church; but this grant was never made, owing, doubtless, to the troubles of the time; for when Sacheverell, Governer of Man, visited Iona in 1688, the buildings were in ruins. 'Though they have no minister,' he tells us, 'they constantly assemble in the great church on Sundays, where they spend most of the day in private devotions.'

By 1693, when Iona passed from the Macleans to the Campbells, all the religious buildings were ruinous, including St. Ronan's Church beside the Nunnery – the mediaeval parish church. For nearly two centuries until 1828, Iona was a holy place without a pastor or a well found place of worship. The only Scottish cathedral to come into private ownership at the Reformation, it was not attacked, but merely neglected. From time to time in the eighteenth century the Argyll estates tried to prevent raiding of the ruins for stone for walls, and secular use as a sheepfold. Visitors in search of the antique and the picturesque came in increasing numbers, and the ordinary lay folk of the island emerge into history for the first time.

Dr. Johnson was told in 1722 that nobody on Iona spoke English; the Statutes of Iona of 1609 that required chiefs' successors to be able to 'read, write and speak Inglis' did not apply to their tenants. However, the good doctor was probably wrong, as so many casual statements about Iona have been, since islander's petitions of one kind or another survive, signed, in English. In 1828 Iona and the adjoining part of the Ross of Mull were made into a *quoad sacra* parish (a parish for purposes of worship) and a

Iona's Book of Benefactors – the millenium page which commemorates an achievement fitting for Columba's home, one thousand years of peace on the island.

The beautiful Nunnery ruins, a permanent work team of local men was established by the Cathedral Trustees to conserve these and restore other buildings with the proceeds of appeals in 1979 and 1985.

REILEAG DRAIN
BURIAL GROUND OF ST ORAN

A view of The Reilig Odhrain with grave slabs, depicted by Graham c. 1850.

The Sacristy Door in 1856, when it was in a sorry state of repair, it has now been fully restored to its former splendour.

'Parliamentary kirk' and manse one of many pairs built in remote parts of the highlands with a Government grant, were erected between the Abbey and the Nunnery.

During the following generation the population peaked and fell away, while at the same time renewed interest in the Abbey and its associations brought over more visitors. Some were souvenir hunters, and others well-meaning in their vandalism. Local people were reported to have scrubbed exposed tombstones for a visit by the Duke of Argyll in 1807, an oriental traveller called Wilson went digging for tombstones in the royal burial ground in 1830, and three years later the Iona Club of Edinburgh met on the island and exposed several more to the element. Gradually the notion of preserving and restoring the beauties of the Iona heritage, rather than mourning their passage, began to gain ground.

In 1874 the eighth Duke of Argyll put in hand a major consolidation of the ruins, and in 1899 he established the Iona Cathedral Trust 'in connection with the Established Church of Scotland' but excluding the parish minister and kirk session from any part in the management; he declared it his wish that the Cathedral (better known as the Abbey church) should be re-roofed and restored and, with unusual tolerance for his time, hoped that the Trustees would occasionally allow members of other Christian Churches to hold services there as well. The Trustees are five office-holders in the Church of Scotland and one each from the four Scottish universities that existed in 1899.

Restoration has proceeded in stages. The rebuilding of the church was completed by 1910 in two instalments. For nearly thirty years it was used by the local congregation as the 1828 parish church became dilapidated; the latter was restored in 1939. The nettle still 'shed her snows above kings' heads', and the thistle 'waved where bishops' mitres stood', but the 'long sleep' which appeared to outsiders to have fallen on the island was now at an end, and there was a general stirring.

An Episcopal chapel had been consecrated in 1894 in the newly built 'St. Columba's House' – known locally as the Bishop's house – a house of retreat for clergy and laity. After the First World War a scheme was floated, with American backing, for a Gaelic college, but it did not materialise. In 1931 Sir David Russell commissioned plans for restoring much of the monastic buildings as a study and retreat centre for theological students and clergy of the Church of Scotland. This too hung fire for seven years until in 1938 the Rev. Dr. George MacLeod (now the Very Rev. Lord MacLeod of Fuinary) founded the Iona Community.

To begin with the Community was conceived as a company of craftsmen and trainee ministers devoted to Christian witness and the practical task of rebuilding the rest of the Abbey. The membership was soon broadened to include men from other backgrounds, and eventually women as well. They accept certain common disciplines of prayer and sharing, and are supported by friends and associates in many countries.

Lord MacLeod became, during the next half century, one of the dominant figures of modern Scotland. His immense energy and eloquence and his ingenuity in attracting interest in the work of the Community – not only on the island but among the poor folk of Glasgow and Edinburgh – have made him a legend in his lifetime. The Community celebrated his ninetieth birthday in 1985 by launching an appeal for the new MacLeod Centre which now stands on a knoll above the Abbey, greatly increasing the Community's capacity to put up visitors for a season of Iona tranquillity and a taste of 'the common life . . . the only key to the world problem' for which the Community has always stood.

In 1959–63 the Community and the Cathedral Trust co-operated in a successful appeal for funds to complete the restoration, finally achieved in 1965. Another interval followed, a period of small works and embellishments, island life continuing its even tenor – until the Argyll Estates put Iona on the market in 1978. A year later the Hugh Fraser Foundation bought it for the nation in memory of Lord Fraser of Allander, and the Government put it in the care of the National Trust for Scotland. The Cathedral Trustees, with the proceeds of appeals in 1979 and 1985, established a permanent work squad of local men, embarked on a major programme of repointing the Abbey and consolidating the beautiful Nunnery ruins, and began fresh work of display and interpretation of the memorials.

Finally, when the declining membership on Iona and Mull moved the Church of Scotland to dispense with a resident parish minister, local people and their friends were given a lease of the manse to develop an Iona Heritage Centre and overnight accommodation for a visiting minister. The message of the few folk in the corner of a remote island, mocked at the Synod of Whitby all these centuries ago, once again goes out radiant and clear as ever.

*T*he Abbey, despite
the amount of
rebuilding which has been
done the whole retains a
dignified homogeneity –
largely through the use of
local materials.

Chapter Seven

THE ANTIQUITIES

The cursory visitor to Iona will probably limit attention to the ecclesiastical treasures held by the Cathedral Trust – the Abbey church and monastic buildings, the Nunnery, the infirmary museum displaying St. John's Cross and the mediaeval effigies, the St. Oran's and Michael chapels, the ancient burial ground of Reilig Odhrain, and the sculpted stones and crosses. The hardy day-tripper may also manage to ascend Dùn-I, the highest point of the island, with a marvellous view in fine weather as recompense for a small exertion, or make a brisk walk to the Machair and the western shore, where the play of light and colour reflects the unceasing movement of the ocean. For those with leisure and interest there is much else.

MACLEAN'S CROSS On the road from the village to the Cathedral, on the spot, it is said, where Columba rested half-way on the last day of his life, there stands a wayside cross carved from a thin slab of chlorite schist, ten feet high above its pedestal. On its western side, the central figure is a crucified Christ in a long robe; a fleur-de-lys is above, and a chalice is on one side. The shaft is adorned with foliage and the interlacing that is characteristic of Celtic ornament. The west side has an ornamental pattern, and below are two animals and a mounted knight with helmet and lance. The cross is believed to date from the last quarter of the fifteenth century and probably commemorates a MacLean of Duart, the dominant family in the district at that time.

THE ABBEY CHURCH stands near the centre of the area bounded by the earthworks within which the Celtic monastery stood. The early Christian crosses sited to the west, and the Columban foundations of the little chapel beside the west door, make it probable that this was the site of the Columban church as well. Mediaeval sources referring to the Abbey consistently call it the 'monastery of St. Columba', and the soubriquet 'St. Mary's Abbey' which was popular at the turn of the century is a misnomer based on reports of early travellers.

There are substantial remains of the original Romanesque structure, but more of the surviving mediaeval masonry dates from the fifteenth-century rebuilding, and the west front in the twentieth-century restoration is a wholly contemporary conception echoing the window pattern of St. Machar's Cathedral in Aberdeen. The circular pier-arch, as Ferguson points out, 'is used with the mouldings of the thirteenth century, and the pointed arch is placed on a capital of intertwined dragons, more worthy of a Runic cross or tombstone than a Gothic edifice. The tower windows are filled with quatrefoil tracery, in a manner very unusual, and mode of construction adopted which does not perhaps exist anywhere else in Britain.'

The building is cruciform, measuring 148 feet 7 inches from east to west and 70 feet 3 inches from north to south, with a massive square tower 70 feet high. The tower may have been completed with a spire, but no record of its form exists, if there was one. Despite the amount of rebuilding, the whole retains a dignified homogeneity, largely through the use of the same materials – local flagstone, granite from the Ross of Mull and, in the form of erratic blocks and glacial boulders, from Iona itself. Greyish-yellow sandstone from Carsaig on the south coast of Mull has been used abundantly for the dressed masonry of plinths, buttresses and openings. A number of masons' marks have been found – some from the thirteenth and some from the fifteenth century – and on one of the column heads is the inscription (in Latin) 'Donaldus O'Brolchan did this work'; the O'Brolchans were a celebrated family of masons and carvers who came to the West Highlands from Donegal.

Other details of interests within the building are the capitals of the tower piers and of the pillars, which are carved with a curious medley of subjects: foliage, grotesque monsters, groups of men and beasts, and Biblical subjects; the carved Gothic sedilia; the tombs of John MacKinnon, the abbot who completed the fifteenth-century rebuilding, and his successor Kenneth Mackenzie, north and south of the sanctuary, and the modern effigies of the eighth Duke of Argyll and his last Duchess. A screen at the north transept was a gift from the Queen after her visit in 1956. (Although many ancient Celtic kings are reputed to be buried on Iona, this was the first attested visit of a reigning monarch since the expedition of Magnus Barelegs to assert his Norwegian sovereignty in 1098.)

On display near the ducal effigies is a photographic reproduction of the Book of Kells, now in Trinity College Library, Dublin, but almost certainly begun and perhaps completed on Iona before the Viking raids;

some of the ornament matches closely that of the high crosses, particularly St. John's. Inside the west door on the north side is displayed the book of benefactors of Iona (*Luchd-taic na h-I*) initiated by the Trustees to mark a thousand years of peace in 1986. On the south wall grave slabs of other mediaeval clergy are now displayed after some years in the infirmary museum. To appreciate the full marvel of this jewel of the Hebrides – the greatest church building in the isles – requires repeated visits, in a storm or in stillness, in company or in solitude, as the thousand variations of Atlantic light, winds wild and gentle in turn and the swell and subsiding of the music of humanity interplay as they have always done for pilgrims down the centuries.

ST. COLUMBA'S SHRINE On the north side of the west entrance to the church is a small and very ancient oratory, now rebuilt and and called St. Columba's Shrine. It contains two stone cists of which the greater, on the south side, traditionally held the shrine of Columba; they have no datable characteristics, but the fact that their bases are at a level similar to the late mediaeval paving west of the chapel indicates that they are probably contemporary. They are now covered by the modern wooden floor. In fact, the shrine in which Columba's remains were placed in the eighth century would have stood in the principal church. There is an older tradition, recorded over three hundred years ago, that this was the site of the saint's tomb or 'monument'. Other evidence gives it a ninth or tenth century date, and it is probably the 'small church of Columcille' mentioned in a Norse saga of the visit of Magnus in 1098.

THE ANCIENT CROSSES Facing the west wall of the Abbey church there stand in line the High Cross of St. Martin, which has apparently stood where it was set for over 1200 years, an impressive replica of the High Cross of St. John, and what remains of the later and smaller Cross of St. Matthew. The original St. John's Cross, restored in 1990 for the third time, is now displayed in the museum, as are the recumbent remaining portions of the High Cross of St. Oran, the oldest of all. With the Kildalton and Kilnave Crosses on Islay, they form an experimental group, carved probably in the eighth century when Iona had recovered its confidence and influence after the humiliation of the Synod of Whitby. Of the sculptors we know nothing. We do not even know the identity of the abbot in whose time these astonishing crosses were conceived and erected.

Sue Anderson

In the distance the village, which lies on the east coast of the island – close to the Abbey and its environs – and faces the island of Mull.

But there is good reason to suppose that St. John's is the first of the Celtic free-standing ringed crosses and that, like the name 'Iona', its development was a happy accident.

Adamnan records three crosses on Iona in his day, carved no doubt in wood and marking important incidents in the life of Columba. But workmanship in stone was rare and simple, mostly grave markers and perhaps travelling pulpit markers (see below). It was not until the Northumbrians, drawing on models and perhaps craftsmen from the Mediterranean, had erected their great crosses like Bewcastle and Ruthwell that Iona turned to ambitious working in stone – and it was ambitious indeed.

First the Family of Hy produced the St. Oran's Cross – massive ringless, made of two sorts of schist available not far away on the Ross of Mull, and with its separate parts held in place like the parts of the Northumbrian crosses by mortice-and-tenon, the woodworker's

The surviving part of St. Martin's Cross photographed in 1986.

technique. Next they conceived the St. John's Cross, unmatched in the splendour of its adornment among Celtic crosses and excelled in height and range by but one in Ireland. It was placed closest to what we now call 'St. Columba's Shrine', and it was carved from greenish-grey chlorite-schist from quarries in mid-Argyll (perhaps Loch Sween) – another indication of the importance attached to the sculpting, requiring several tons of stone to be brought across the two Sounds, no doubt on rafts. This cross, too, was constructed with mortice-and-tenon, the shaft in one solid piece, the crosshead in another, and a small lower arm (now entirely lost) connecting the two.

The result was carving of great beauty, but structural weakness. Examination of the stonework since 1960 suggests an early fall, after which a ring in four pieces, two supporting the crosshead from below and two completing their harmonious whole above, was carved out of silver-grey mica-schist from Mull. A further extension of the crosshead and a crest were added from the same material. We do not know how long the cross stood after that, but in modern times only a small part of the shaft survived on its original base. The elements of the rest of the cross were identified and reassembled in the nineteenth century, and in 1927 the whole was raised again on its original base with concrete patching. The upper part was

Sue Anderson

MacLean's Cross, this monument is believed to date from the last quarter of the fifteenth century and probably commemorates a MacLean of Duart.

blown down in a gale in 1951, re-erected in 1954 and shattered again in 1957. Eventually the Trustees had the pieces removed for conservation and in 1970 the replica was cast in concrete from the moulds of George Mancini, who was able to copy all but a tiny portion of the decoration of the crosshead from the original. In 1990 the original cross was reassembled again and erected in the sheltered setting of the Abbey museum.

St. Martin's Cross was carved from a single piece of epidiorite, probably from one of the adjacent islands, which permits less refinement of carving than the main part of St. John's. The ring is smaller and the arms are relatively stubby, but there are slots into which extensions, probably made of wood, may have been inserted on special occasions. In modern times it has been cleaned of great accumulations of lichen, and carries the robust dignity of the one high cross that has weathered the ages on Iona. On Islay the Kildalton Cross, similar in outline to St. John's but carved from a single piece of epidiorite like St. Martin's, is also intact.

Within a lifetime from the raising of the crosses, the Iona flowering was rudely ended by the Viking raids. It seems likely that St. Matthew's Cross was carved some time in the late ninth or early tenth century; it was a relatively short monolithic cross of a type common in Ireland at that period; the sculpture is much less dexterous than on the other crosses and the coarse grey sandstone of which it is composed made both elegance and survival difficult. It may have been erected by way of thanksgiving for the return of peace to Iona as the Northmen embraced Christianity.

THE BLACK STONES OF IONA Near the same spot there once stood one of the most ancient and revered of Iona's relics – the Black Stones of Iona, so called not from their colour but from the black doom that fell on any who dared to violate an oath sworn upon them. As recently as the reign of James VI and I, two clans foreswore a long-standing blood feud and pledged themselves to friendship by the Black Stones.

There was a tradition, now thoroughly exploded, that the Coronation Stone in Westminster Abbey was one of the Black Stones. The fanciful history, whose origin is unknown, claimed that it was revered as Jacob's pillow by the tribes who brought it from the East in the waves of Celtic migration. 'On this stone – the old Druidic Stone of Destiny, sacred among the Gael before Christ was born – Columba crowned Aidan King of Argyll,' wrote Fiona Macleod. 'Later the stone was taken to Dunstaffnage, where the Lords of the Isles were made princes: thence to

Scone, where the last of the Celtic Kings of Scotland were crowned on it. It now lies in Westminster Abbey, a part of the Coronation Chair, and since Edward I every British monarch has been crowned upon it. If ever the Stone of Destiny be moved again, that writing on the wall will be the signature of a falling dynasty.'

It is now forty years since the Stone was removed and returned, without noticeable prejudice to the House of Windsor; the style of Lord of the Isles hardly predated Edward I and his castle was in Islay, not at Dunstaffnage; there is no evidence that the Druids revered stones or that Celtic tribes were ever near Palestine in the course of the migrations, and the Stone of Destiny appears to be local Perthshire stone. But like so much else conjectured about Iona, it makes a good story.

ST. COLUMBA'S PILLOW Adamnan in his Life of Columba refers to the saint's bed 'where he had a bare flagstone for his couch, and for his pillow a stone, which stands to this day as a kind of monument beside his grave.' About 1870 the tenant of Clachanach, the croft immediately north of the Abbey, dug up a troublesome stone which struck the wheel of his cart at the entrance to a field. It turned out to be an oval-shaped boulder with a ringed cross incised on it. Who first took it to be Columba's Pillow is unknown, but it became so popular and widely accepted that for many

A nineteenth-century view of the island, St. Oran's Chapel and the Abbey taken in 1856.

The replica of St. John's Cross which now stands in line with St. Martin's and St. Matthew's crosses facing the west wall of the Abbey.

Scottish Conservation Partnership

The High Cross of St. John, it was restored in 1990 for the third time and is now suitably housed in the shelter of the Infirmary museum.

years the stone was displayed in the sanctuary of the Abbey church. It is now in the museum.

THE MONASTERY The mediaeval monastic buildings adjoin the Abbey church to the north. There is a square cloister, somewhat altered in the fifteenth century at the time of rebuilding the church, and two of the original sandstone columns survive. The chapter-house is on the east, the refectory to the north and the kitchen and main entrance on the west. Near the refectory stands the restored Abbot's house, connected with the Abbey through the reredorter. The restored cloister arcades, modelled on the thirteenth-century cloister, were completed in 1959, and the capitals have been carved with representations of plants and birds from Europe and North America. There is a large bronze sculpture representing 'the Descent of the Spirit' in the middle of the garth; the work of the Lithuanian sculptor Jacques Lipchitz, it includes in its modernistic styling the specifically Columban symbol of the dove. The Iona Community, restorers of these buildings, now occupy them as rent-free tenants of the Cathedral Trust and act as custodians of the Abbey church; the east and west ranges provide accommodation for guests all the year round.

THE MICHAEL CHAPEL A small church east of the monastic buildings, which is only 33 feet by 16 feet, may have been used by the early Benedictines for worship while the main Abbey church was being built. It was beautifully restored in 1959 by the Iona Community, who use it for winter worship, and the name dates from that time, although there is a record of a chapel or burial-vault dedicated to St. Michael in the sixteenth century, and they may well be the same.

THE INFIRMARY MUSEUM In 1938, when the Iona Community was founded, there was a small enclosed space, about 53 feet by 17 feet, north of the ruins that became the Michael Chapel. The remains of a wall, to a uniform height of about two feet, surrounded it, and it was assumed to be all that was left of the infirmary for sick and aged mediaeval monks. Twenty years later, concerned about the continued damage that hard weather was causing to the memorial stones in the royal burial ground and elsewhere, the Trustees proposed to rebuild the infirmary as a museum; with a grant from the Carnegie United Kingdom Trust and joint funding by the Trustees and the Community, it was completed in the style of the

The Kildalton Cross of Islay, carved from a single piece of epidiorite like St. Martin's and similar in outline to St. John's, survives intact.

Dennis Hardley

other restorations in 1964, and for a quarter of a century housed most of the memorial stones that had not been totally eroded. In 1990, to house the restored St. John's Cross and display St. Oran's Cross, the building was converted into its present form internally, with the bulk of the memorial stones redistributed about the Abbey and its precincts. Five massive effigies from the late mediaeval period on the north wall remind the visitor of the second period of Iona art in the noble shadow of the Church of St. Columba. A number of early Christian incised stones and early and late mediaeval cross shafts are also on display, as well as the well loved memorial of Prioress Anna Maclean (sixteenth century) with her lapdogs, pending the development of a suitably sheltered setting at the Nunnery, where it originally lay.

THE CELTIC MONASTERY The location and extent of the original enclosures in which St. Columba's monastery lay have been reasonably accurately determined by modern research – about twenty acres delimited by the earthwork or *vallum* which may still be clearly seen west of the road north of the present Abbey grounds. The Celtic monastery consisted ordinarily of a group of small churches dominated by a round tower which served as a belfry and lookout station and surrounded by individual cells of wattle-and-daub construction. However, Adamnan describes only one church building in Columba's monastery with an annex or attached chamber. The grouping of the three high crosses suggests that by the eighth century the church was situated close to the site of the mediaeval Abbey church – perhaps on the same site. What was claimed in 1908 to be the foundations of a round tower twenty feet west of the Abbey church was shown in 1976 to be in fact an area of undisturbed late mediaeval paving.

Few traces remain of the series of buildings described by Adamnan, apart from some post-holes, the remains of drainage ditches, and quantities of animal and fish bones which indicate that Columba's noted austerity did not extend to the diet of his colleagues and guests. Pollen samples indicate that oak and ash grew in the neighbourhood in the sixth century – perhaps one of the initial attractions of the site – although Adamnan also describes wood being floated across from Mull in his day.

THE ROYAL BURIAL GROUND (REILIG ODHRAIN) The ancient burying-ground of Reilig Odhrain lies, 'weel biggit about with staine and lime', a little south-west of the Abbey church. It has been in continuous use from time immemorial, and although this contributes to the reverential thrill of contemplating it, it has made excavation impossible and so determination of its former extent problematical. One speculation for which there is some written evidence is that religious were buried hard by the Abbey and laymen, nobility and gentry, princes and chiefs, in the area in and about the present burial ground. After the foundation of the Nunnery, religious women seem to have been buried in its precincts, and the ordinary folk of Iona in early and mediaeval times may have been buried in one or other of the cemeteries outside the monastic precincts altogether.

The tradition that ancient kings lie here is more than 800 years old, but there is no contemporary evidence that the entire House of Alpin, from Kenneth, first King of Picts and Scots (died 860) to Macbeth (died 1058) were interred in the Reilig Odhrain. By 1549 Dean Monro could report the tradition that sixty kings were buried on Iona, 48 of Scotland and the other from Norway and Ireland, and one from France. It is certainly true that this 'awful ground', as Dr. Johnson called it, includes the graves of a great company of Hebridean and West Highland chiefs. The peace of a thousand years whispers over their resting place, and the thoughtful visitor is filled with the sense of wonder inspired by the fact of morality against the gleaming canvas of the ever-moving Sound, the great cliffs of Mull and the wide skyscape from the Atlantic to the distant mountains.

In such surroundings the fancy plays, as it has always done. History and myth run together, sometimes indicating that old superstitions and missionary religion may run together as well. They are so deeply embedded in the lore of Iona that a guide would be incomplete that ignored them. The oldest of such myths states that it was revealed to St. Columba that a human sacrifice would be necessary for the success of his mission. His cousin, Oran, one of the original twelve who accompanied him to Iona, offered himself and was buried alive. On the third day Columba ordered the grave to be opened, whereupon Oran opened his eyes and said: 'Death is no wonder, nor is hell as it is said.' Such heresy was not pleasing to the saint's ear, and his reply: 'Earth, earth on Oran's eye, lest he further blab', has passed into a proverb. However, Oran's name does not appear in the earliest surviving list of Columba's companions, and the

*T*he cloister which
contains a sculpture
by Jacques Lipchitz, 'The
Descent of the Spirit' in
the middle of the Garth –
it includes, in modernistic
styling, Columba's symbol
of the dove.

*I*ona Abbey and Dùn-I
from the sound of
Mull, showing the
Michael Chapel which
was restored by the Iona
Community in 1959, the
name dates from the
restoration.

*I*ona Abbey and the
Street of the Dead,
although the tradition that
the ancient kings are
buried on the island is
over 800 years old there
is no absolute proof, but it
is certain that a great
many Hebridean and
West Highland chiefs are.

legend receives no support from Adamnan's account of the first funeral among the Family of Hy, nor can we be sure that it was in this ground.

In simpler days, besides, there was an assumption that even a sinner buried close to a saint might manage to heaven on the holy man's coat tails, and as late as the middle of the last century some islanders had themselves buried under existing grave slabs. An ancient prophecy offered another reason for choosing Iona:

> *Seven years before the judgment,*
> *The sea shall sweep over Erin at one side,*
> *And over blue-green Islay;*
> *But I of Colum of the Church shall*
> *swim.*

The repute of royal burials reached Shakespeare by way of Holinshed's chronicles:

> *Ross.* Where is Duncan's body?
> *Macduff.*   Carried to Colme-kill,
>   The sacred storehouse of his predecessors,
> And guardian of their bones.

Some small mortuary-houses, similar to those which still survive in some Irish churchyards, were described by visitors up to the eighteenth century, and they appear to have had later inscriptions describing them as tombs of Kings of Scotland, Ireland and Norway. Some at least of them may have dated back to the twelfth century.

Most of the memorial stones on Iona originally lay in the Reilig Odhrain and, as we have seen, suffered erosion and wanton damage of one kind or another over the centuries. In 1859 the eighth Duke of Argyll enclosed several of the finest of them within iron railings in two parallel rows, the 'Ridge of the Kings' and the 'Ridge of the Chiefs'. After the rebuilding of the mediaeval infirmary as a museum in 1964, most of the stones that were not totally defaced were temporarily stored there until their redistribution in 1990.

ST. ORAN'S CHAPEL Within the burial ground is a small chapel, 29 feet by 15 feet in dimension and known as St. Oran's Chapel. It is the oldest of the surviving mediaeval buildings, but not old enough to have been the gift of Queen Margaret in the late eleventh century. It was probably put up by either Somerled or his son Reginald a couple of generations later as a mortuary chapel for their family, and some of their descendants were almost certainly interred there. It is nowadays a plain, quiet place, simply furnished, but in its heyday its plaster walls would have been richly decorated, and the late mediaeval tomb recess that occupies about a third of the total length of the south wall carries an aura of lost grandeur. The doorway has an elaborately carved arch-head which appears to be of a style later than that of the rest of the building, and inserted shortly afterwards. A striking feature of the modern chapel is the polished steel cross on the east wall which catches the eye of the visitor through the open door, and in ordinary daylight the beams and other structural features cast a shadow on the east wall which seems in the form of a cross.

For many years the composite lid of an early Christian cross-base, later moved to the Abbey museum, lay near the edge of the path to St. Oran's Chapel. It was known as the clach-brath (judgment stone), and pilgrims as late as the nineteenth century turned small stones in the cavity sunwise for personal divination or a view of the end of the world. It was commonly believed that the Day of Judgment would not come about until this stone should be worn through.

THE NUNNERY Like the Abbey, the Nunnery was established at the beginning of the thirteenth century – on a raised beach about a quarter of mile from the Abbey and close to the jetty at St. Ronan's Bay. Most of the surviving parts date back to the thirteenth century, although there were alterations towards the end of the fifteenth to provide a more spacious cloister garth. The church, partially restored in 1923, and portions of the convent buildings on the south side compose one of the best preserved nunneries of its type in the British Isles. The walls were consolidated during the works commissioned by the Duke of Argyll in 1874 but remain in a precarious condition, made worse by the heavy traffic for recent building works at the Abbey and the MacLeod Centre. A number of fine sculptured pieces, including memorials of two prioresses and other religious ladies, mediaeval and early modern, are currently displayed elsewhere until work on the fabric is completed.

The masonry is composed of red granite interspersed with courses of flagstone and basalt rubble, with dressings of greenish-yellow Carsaig sandstone which has not weathered well, so that nearly all the early carvings and mouldings have badly deteriorated. Consolidation has required the removal of the riotous plant growth, mostly toadflax and valerian, which made the ruins a beautiful blaze of colour the summer long, but ate into the mortar. A serious frost in 1980 – a very rare event on Iona – did further damage. The garth has been intermittently cultivated as a garden for the last sixty years or so. Occasional proposals to restore the Nunnery, like early proposals to restore the Abbey, have constantly foundered on the question of what use could be found for it.

SCULPTURED STONES Apart from the high crosses, there are more than a hundred early Christian stones on Iona, including a dozen other free-standing crosses ranging from complete examples to small fragments; two are of Scandinavian character. Within the total there are several distinct groups – primitive and very simple incised crosses, probably early grave markers, but some shaped like inverted spearheads that inspire the notion that they may have been carried on missionary expeditions, and driven into the ground at a preaching station.

An illustration of the memorial to Dr. John Beaton, depicted by Graham c. 1850.

Abundant and (in some examples) skilful though the early Christian sculptures are, there does not appear to have been what could have been called a 'school' of sculpture in the Columban period. The high crosses might have presaged one, had it not been for the Viking disasters. Working in stone in the centuries of eclipse between 800 and 1200 was, so far as we can tell, occasional and frequently by alien hands, or at least on alien models. The three centuries rule by the family of Somerled gave patronage and protection to a distinctive Iona School, responsible for 64 of the eighty-two grave slabs which survive in the island with detectable ornament – swords and galleys and curiously intertwined foliage patterns.

The effigies represent five warriors, five abbots and a prior. The work of the Iona school fell away with the forfeiture of the Lordship of the Isles in 1493 and two of the three most notable carvings of the early sixteenth century – the effigy of John MacIán of Ardnamurchan and the memorial of Prioress Anna MacLean – were the product of the Oronsay school.

Among later pieces the most interesting celebrates the life and labours of Dr. John Beaton, one of the learned kindred of Mac a'bheatha (in the southern isles and Ireland) or Mac beathhadh (in the north) who practised medicine in Gaelic Scotland for some four centuries. The name (literally, 'son of life') was anglicised to Beaton in the seventeenth century when it

*N*owadays St.
Oran's chapel is a
plain, quiet place but
formerly its walls would
have been richly decorated
and its silhouette provokes
images of lost grandeur.

*T*he grave slab of
MacDonald of Islay
(fifteenth century), drawn
by H. D. Graham
c. 1850.

was expedient for anyone following a profession to do so in 'Inglis'. He died in 1657. A few miles to the east in the Ross of Mull, clearly visible from the road to Iona, stands a wayside cross with the initials GMB and DMB – Gille-calum MacBheatha and son Domhall, Dr. John's great-grandfather. The memorials are a pleasant reminder of a society more advanced in the arts of peace (as well as war) than we sometimes believe. The doctors were not related to the much maligned King Macbeth, who may or may not also lie in hopes of salvation on Iona. In his day it was a forename, which appears to have died out by 1200.

ST. RONAN'S CHURCH Probably the mediaeval parish church, this little building, some 35 feet by 15 feet, stands in the Nunnery precints immediately north of the nuns' church. It is built of random rubble with dressings of sandstone, but much of its original structure is unknown. It was restored in 1923 and given a glass roof to house carved stones, and the Cathedral Trustees have announced their intention to equip it as a scholar's museum for the study of stones and fragments of specialist interest.

The first reference to the parish church of Iona that survives records the appointment by the Pope of a new rector in 1372. The last resident minister before the building of the Parliamentary kirk departed in 1661. It is not known when the use of St. Ronan's for worship was discontinued; it was reported as 'intire but tottering' in 1795 and was completely ruinous by 1874.

Chapter Eight

TOPOGRAPHY

By far the greater number of visitors to Iona spend only a few hours on the island, and as a rule their time is fully occupied in the inspection of the antiquities described in the previous chapter. Full of interest as these are, people whose attention is thus confined are apt to carry away an impression not so much of the Iona of Columba as of the mediaeval Iona, in the relatively uneventful era of the Benedictine occupation. 'It is rather the fair sea-beauty and imaginative charm of the place that links us with the ancient, simple days of material poverty and spiritual fruitfulness,' says Trenholme.

In order to get at this Iona, it is essential to make a stay on the island. With the pressure of visitors, this is more difficult than it used to be, and advance booking is advisable for any time between May and October. There are two hotels and a boarding house, as well as the Iona Community accommodation at the Abbey and the MacLeod Centre, and many of the cottages make provision for visitors.

This chapter is specially intended for those who have leisure to appreciate the manifold attractions of the little island. It is not within the compass of a small handbook to deal in a detailed way with even the history and antiquities of the island, much less its geology, natural history, and other aspects. The specialist will have recourse to the standard authorities, and for others who desire to extend their knowledge in any particular aspect, a small bibliography is appended. With leisure, the imaginative will be able to linger in the quiet places beloved of Columba and his followers, and to spirit themselves into the dim past; the artist will discover the beauty of the atmospheric effects; the antiquarian will find fresh fields of interest; the nature lover will be absorbed in the varieties of bird, and flower, and stone; the rambler can wander at will over moorland and rock and sheeny sand; and many pleasing trips can be made to the entrancing islets that surround Iona.

In this chapter, the places of special interest in Iona will be enumerated and briefly annotated. Beginning just north of the Abbey Church, the route followed will run roughly in a counter-sunwise direction.

ST. COLUMBA'S CELL The Saint's private cell stood a little apart from the centre of monastic life. The clues given in Adamnan all point to Tor Abb, but the exact spot remained a matter of speculation until the summer of 1957, when the summit was stripped and a cell revealed that conforms to all the evidence we have. It lay beneath a ridge 'like a cow's backbone,' and its low stone walls, 'carefully keyed into irregularities in the living rock,' and no more than a few feet high, were surmounted by stubs of small wooden stakes, in the form of charcoal. This suggested a kind of wigwam construction of wood, turf, heather and thatch for the roof. Within the cell was a broad slab of rock that could serve as a seat or bed. *'Pro stramine nudam petram, et pro pullvillo lapidem,'* wrote Adamnan of Columba – for mattress the bare rock, and for pillow a stone. In so far as the archaeologists will commit themselves without positive evidence, and unless evidence to the contrary is ever brought to light, this will be accepted as the veritable cell of the Saint.

THE LOCHAN MÓR (the Great Pond), now drained to a bog, was originally the monastery mill-pond, and from it the MILL-STREAM still trickles along its deep bed just north of the Abbey Church to the shore. Adamnan mentions a kiln and a granary in the proximity of the monastery, and Pennant in 1772 saw by the mill-stream 'the ruins of a kiln' (for drying corn) 'and a granary; and near it was the mill.' Traces of buildings still remain on the high road by the mill-stream, west of the road.

CLADH AN DISEIRT (Burial-ground of the Hermitage) or CLADH IAIN (St. John's Cemetery). In a lonely spot a little south-west of the stone Blathnat are two rough granite pillars, which, with a third stone that lay across the top, formed a rude gateway to what was formerly a small enclosure. In 1880, excavators discovered here the foundation of a hermit's cell of the oblong type, 26 feet by 17, facing due east, and having traces of an altar-piece at the east end. These 'disarts' or hermitages were built sometimes in solitary places, sometimes in the neighbourhood of a monastery. The hermits spent their time chiefly in prayer and contemplation, and were frequently sought as spiritual advisers. They studied also, and worked at handicrafts, like other monks.

A hermit was usually buried in or near his cell: hence the name of the ground adjoining this disart.

IONA

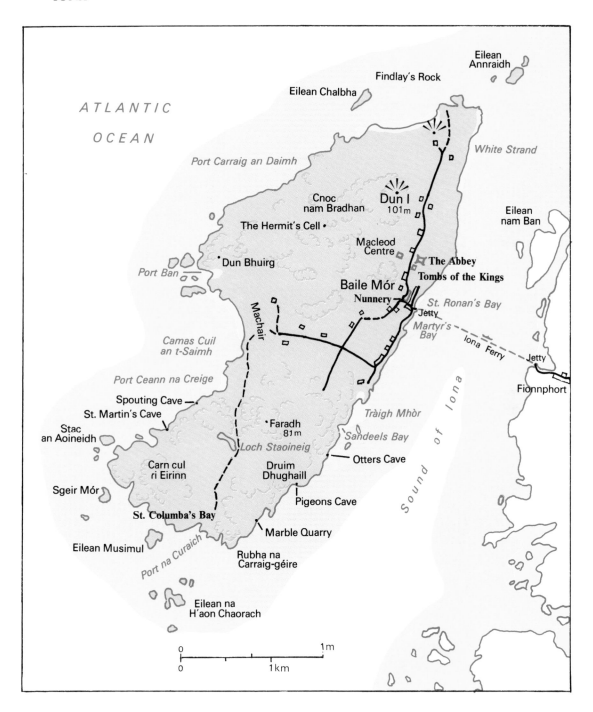

IONA – A HISTORY OF THE ISLAND

THE CAUSEWAY (*Iomair an Tàchair*, Ridge of the Gleaning), or BISHOP'S WALK, is an ancient roadway, 22 feet wide and 220 yards long, built high above the Lochan Mór. Skene suggests that it was constructed by Cillene Droiteach (Cillen the Bridgemaker), the fourteenth Abbot, as a means of communication between the monastery and the Hermit's Cell in the wild, north-west tract of the island. Traces of a roadway connecting the causeway and the Cell are still to be seen.

THE HERMIT'S CELL lies deep in turf and heather, a few yards south-west of Cnoc nam Bradhan (Hill of the Querns). Only the foundation, on which stones have been piled, is left. It is almost circular in shape, and about 18 feet in diameter. The Gaelic name, *Cobhain Cuildich*, is popularly translated Culdee Cell, but this *carcair* – so the Irish call the beehive hut of a hermit – is probably of much greater antiquity than the Culdee order. It is possible that the above-mentioned Cillen, who was an anchorite abbot, ruled the monastery from this spot, and Skene thinks that it may have been originally one of Columba's prayer places. 'It's position looking out over the ocean to Tiree,' says Trenholme, 'suits Adamnan's description of the place among the bushes, remote from men, and meet for prayer, where Columba went to pray one day and beheld (perhaps in a storm of thunder and lightning) hosts of demons fighting with darts in the sky, above Iona, but at last driven off to Tiree.'

Traces of a walled walk, ascending to and enclosing the hillock, are mentioned in the *Statistical Account* published a hundred years ago, but the last vestiges seem to have disappeared.

WELL OF THE NORTH WIND (*Tobair na Gaoithe Tuath*). This is one of the magic wells of antiquity. It lies north of Cnoc nam Bradhan, not far from the Hermit's Cell. Here, in olden times, sailors and others brought offerings to charm up a wind from the north. A well of the south wind traditionally exists in Iona, but can no longer be traced.

DÙN-I (Hill, or Hill-Fortress of I), the one hill of Iona, lies immediately behind the Abbey Church. Ascent can be made from any side, but the best route from the village ascends just behind Clachanach. There is an old superstition that good luck follows those who have made the ascent seven times. A cairn marks the summit, where possibly an island fortress once stood.

TOPOGRAPHY

On a clear day, a vast expanse of hill and sea and sky is revealed, and a sunset or, better, a sunrise seen from Dùn-I is a thing not to be forgotten. The principal islands within sight of the summit are enumerated in the first chapter, and in the last there is quoted an impression of Iona from the slopes of Dùn-I, by Fiona Macleod.

THE WELL OF YOUTH OR POOL OF HEALING (*Tobair na h'Aoise*, Well of the Age). On the northern brow of Dùn-I, half hidden by an overhanging rock, there lies a small triangular pool, the fame of which used to be far spread. Here, through ages past, pilgrims of each generation have lingered at the enchanted hour of dawn, 'to touch the healing water the moment the first sunray quickens it.' So they thought to recover their lost youth: some, perhaps, its physical strength and beauty; others its dreams and aspirations.

THE WHITE SANDS skirt the north-western shore. They are of unusual whiteness, and are composed of the powdered shells of innumerable land-snails. The stretch of sand known as *Tràigh Bhàn nam Manach* (White Strand of the Monks) is believed to have been the scene of the third slaughter of Iona monks by the Danes, and the dark, steep rock at the northern extremity is said to have been stained with the blood of the victims.

DUN CUL BHUIRG On a steep rocky slope overlooking the western sea, this Iron Age Fort was extensively excavated in 1957, 1959 and 1968. A few scraps of pottery and some beads were found, helping to date the settlement between 100 BC and AD200. It is the oldest authenticated evidence of human settlement on the island. There are no records, either written or archaeological, of the population when Columba arrived, if there was any. The tradition that it was a Druidic place of pilgrimage is of a much later date.

GLEANN AN TEAMPUILL (Glen of the Church) lies about the middle of the island, north of the Machair. It is believed to be the site of the monastery previously mentioned, which was erected by the Benedictine monks on their taking possession of Iona, and intended, Skene thinks, for the Celtic monks, that they might be out of the way. There was an old burial-ground at the head of the glen, but no traces of it remain.

The north of the island, looking towards Dùn-I, its highest point.

THE MACHAIR (*A' Mhachair*, the Plain) is a tract of arable land in the middle west of the island. Adamnan speaks of Columba's monks as labouring here at the harvest, and it was to this spot that Columba was driven in a cart to tell the brethren of his approaching end.

THE CAMUS (*Camus Cul an t-Saimh*, Bay at the Back of the Ocean) is the name of the long, curving bay that skirts the Machair. Hither it was that Columba sent a monk to tend the wounded crane alighted from Ireland. It has one or two sheltered, sandy inlets that are specially suited for bathing. Poll-eirinn (Pool of Ireland), at the north end of the bay, is believed to have been in later times a smugglers' landing-place.

ANGELS' HILL (in Gaelic *Cnoc nam Aingeal*, but better known locally by its old Gaelic name *Sithean Mór*, great fairy-mound) is a grassy knoll just south of the extremity of the road leading to the Machair. As its ancient

Alba Pictures

name signifies, it is one of the fairy knolls of pre-Christian times, one of several in Iona. In these knolls, they say, the Wee Folk were wont to hold revel, and mortals passing by have heard faint strains of fairy music proceeding from within. But the Angels' Hill has also a special association with Columba; for one day – so Adamnan relates – the saint was seen by a prying monk to ascend this hillock, and as he stood 'praying with hands spread out to heaven; and raising his eyes heavenward, behold! suddenly a marvellous thing appeared, . . . for Holy Angels, citizens of the Celestial Country, clad in white garments, came flying to him with wonderful speed, and stood round the holy man as he prayed; and after some conversation with the blessed man, that heavenly band . . . sped swiftly back to the high heavens.'

The prying monk stood probably on the adjacent mound called Cnoc Odhrain, beside the croft of that name.

In later days, according to Pennant, the Angels' Hill was the scene of a

The famous White Sands of Iona which skirt the north-western coast of the island, they are made up of the shells of land-snails.

general cavalcade at the Feast of St. Michael, the natives coursing round the hilllock, on horseback – a ceremony common throughout the Western Isles; for, says Trenholme, 'Michael of the Snow-white Steed appears with Mary Mother and Kind Columkill in the old songs and hymns of the Islesmen, as a great protector by sea and shore.'

THE SPOUTING CAVE A little south of the Machair is a dark cavern into which the sea enters by a natural tunnel at the base of the rocks, and from which, finding itself trapped, it seeks escape through a cleft or 'blow-hole' in the roof, driving a column of water high above the cliffs. The action can best be seen at high tide, with the wind in the south-west.

CARN CUL RI EIRINN (*The Cairn of-the-Back-to-Erin*) stands on *Druim an Aoinidh* (Ridge of the Cliff) near the south-western extremity of the island. This cairn is believed to mark the spot where Columba scanned the horizon on his arrival in order to be assured that his beloved Erin was out of sight. Among the many poems attributed to Columba, there is one of great beauty that remarkably describes the scene from this spot.

PORT LARAICHEAN (Bay of Ruins) lies near the middle of the southern shore, opposite Eilean Musimul. A little back from the beach, on a grassy terrace of artificial construction, are the foundations of six or seven circular stone huts, with a larger and squarer one on a rock near by. Recent research indicates that they were shellings for summer grazing until modern times.

GARADH EACHAINN OIG (Garden of Young Hector) – the name probably commemorates a MacLean of Duart – at the head of Port na Curaich, and PORT GOIRTEIN IOMHAIR (Bay of Ivor's Garth), farther east, have both traces of little buildings.

PORT A' CHURAICH (Bay of the Coracle), on the southern shore, a little to the east of Port Laraichean, is the historic bay where Columba first landed in Iona with his twelve companions. It is flanked with high rocks, and is divided in two by a low rock islet, which forms a kind of natural pier when the weather and tide are favourable. The east side is Port na Curaich proper.

Columba is said to have buried his coracle on the beach, and a long, grassy mound at the head of the bay was commonly believed to conceal the relic. Recent excavations, however, revealed nothing; and it is now suggested that this is no more than an isolated portion of storm beach.

A number of cairns have been piled up at the western end of the beach. Pennant, who saw a vast tract of them hereabouts, says that they were believed to be the penances of monks. Reeves thinks they are probably sepulchral, and Trenholme suggests that this was the cemetery of the men who lived in Port Laraichean.

The beach below is strewn with coloured pebbles of great variety and beauty, and on a sunny day, when the tide is receding, they sparkle and glow like Eastern gems.

Out in the bay, there is a reef of translucent green serpentine from which tiny fragments are broken off and cast ashore by the waves. These pebbles, which are becoming rarer, are known as Iona stone, or St. Columba's stone, and are reputed to be a charm against drowning.

THE MARBLE QUARRY Reference has been made to the Iona marble, a fine, ornamental stone of white veined with the green of the mineral serpentine, and suited in our climate for internal but not external use. It is 'an ophicalite, resembling the green Connemara marble and the Verde Antico of the ancients' (*The Quarry*, December, 1907). The quarry is at the foot of a ravine, facing the Sound, and not far from the south-western extremity of the island; and its position – shut in as it is by cliff and boulder, and giving on to an inhospitable shore – makes the difficulties of transit almost insurmountable.

PIGEONS' CAVE To reach the Pigeons' Cave, which is at the foot of the next ravine, slightly farther north, the pedestrian should turn down a grassy ravine, just opposite to the Sound of Erraid, and he will find the entrance hidden among the rocks to the right. As its name signifies, the cave is the haunt of the wild pigeon. It is 40 yards long, and has a sandy bottom. There is a second cave beside it, nearer the sea.

LOCH STAONAIG is the name of a marshy loch that one is likely to encounter while crossing the island to explore the southern shore. It lies about the middle of the southern tract.

MARTYRS' BAY lies not far south of the village. On its southern

*T*he remarkable
   Spouting Cave, a
little south of the
Machair, the sea enters by
a natural tunnel at the
base of the rocks and
escapes through a 'blow-
hole'.

*P*ort a' Churaich (Bay of the Coracle) the historic site where St. Columba landed with his twelve companions.

*T*he Bishop's House with haystacks in the foreground, agriculture has long been an important part of life on the island, Fionnphort on Mull is in the background.

promontory stands the little Free Kirk (now a private building) which with its modest dimensions and innocence of art strikes perhaps a more harmonious note than the mediaeval Abbey in the island of Columba. Tradition associates this spot with the first recorded slaughter of the monks by the Danes in 806.

It was to this little port that the galleys and barges of old brought the distinguished dead. Opposite the bay is a low, green mound called Ealadh, and here the bodies were laid for a space, while the mourners gathered round 'to pour their wailing over the dead.'

THE STREET OF THE DEAD This is the traditional name of the road that led from Martyrs' Bay to Reilig Odhrain, and marked the route of the funeral trains of old.

Chapter Nine

CONCLUSION

This, then, is the Iona of Columba.

'There is the bay where the little, sea-tossed coracle drove ashore. There is the hill – the Hill of Angels – where heavenly visitants shone before him. There is the sound across which the men of Mull heard vespers sung by hooded monks – heard the Lord's song sung in a strange land. There is the narrow strip of water across which holy men came to take counsel, sinners to do pennance, kings to be crowned. The little island speaks with a quiet insistence of its past – for was it not at once the fountain and the fortress of the faith, at once the centre of Celtic learning and of Christian charity?' – (Troup.)

'The mountaineer and the fisherman and the shepherd of the Isles live their lives in lonely places, and the winds and waves bear to them messages from the unknown beyond. They hear the tide of Eternity forever breaking round the coasts of time, and in spirit they, like St. Brendan, voyage far in fairy seas . . . .

'Part of the inheritance of the Celt is the sense of the longing and striving after the unattainable and incomprehsnsible on Earth . . . . Forlorn, he has the sense of fighting a losing battle for all his soul holds dear; for the simple life of old, for the beauty of the world threatened with utilitarian desecration, for outlived ideals of love and faith and loyalty, of honour and chivalry.' – (Wilkie.)

'As I write, here on the hill-slope of Dùn-I, the sound of the furtive wave is as the sighing in a shell. I am alone between sea and sky, for there is no other on this bouldered height, nothing visible but a single blue shadow that slowly sails the hill-side. The bleating of the lambs and ewes, the lowing of kine, these come up from the Machair that lies between the west slopes and the shoreless sea to the west; these ascend as the very smoke of the sound. All around the island there is a continuous breathing; deeper and more prolonged on the west, where the open sea is, but audible everywhere. The seals on Soa are even now putting their breasts against the running tide; for I see a flashing of fins here and there in patches at the north end of the Sound, and already from the ruddy granite shores of the Ross there is a congregation of sea-fowl – gannets and guillemots, skuas

Looking towards the sea from the slopes of Dùn-I, one of the views that has inspired people for centuries.

and herring-gulls, the long-necked northern diver, the cormorant. In the sunblaze, the waters of the Sound dance their blue bodies and swirl their flashing white hair o' foam; and, as I look, they seem to me like children of the wind and the sunshine, leaping and running in these flowing pastures, with a laughter as sweet against the ears as the voices of children at play.

'The joy of life vibrates everywhere . . . . Not a stone's throw from where I lie, half-hidden beneath an overhanging rock is the Pool of Healing. To this small, black-brown tarn, pilgrims of every generation, for hundreds of years, have come. Solitary, these; not only because the pilgrim to the Fount of Eternal Youth must fare higher alone, and at dawn, so as to touch the healing water the moment the first sunray quickens it – but solitary, also, because those who go in quest of this Fount of Youth are the dreamers and the Children of Dream, and these are not many, and few come now to this lonely place. Yet an Isle of Dream Iona is, indeed. Here the last sun-worshippers bowed before the rising of God; here Columba

Alba Pictures

and his hymning priests laboured and brooded . . . here, for century after century, the Gael has lived, suffered, joyed, dreamed his impossible, beautiful dream; as here, now, he still lives, still suffers patiently, still dreams, and through all and over all, broods upon the incalculable mysteries. He is an elemental, among the elemental forces. He knows the voices of wind and sea; and it is because the Fount of Youth upon Dùn-I of Iona is not the only well-spring of peace, that the Gael can confront his destiny as he does, and can endure . . . . For the genius of the Celtic race stands out now with averted touch, and the light of it is a glory before the eyes, and the flame of it is blown into the hearts of the stronger people. The Celt fades, but his spirit rises in the heart and the mind of the Anglo-Celtic peoples, with whom are the destinies of generations to come.

'I stop, and look sea-ward from this hill-slope of Dùn-I. Yes, even in this Isle of Joy, as it seems in this dazzle of golden light and splashing wave, there is the like mortal gloom and immortal mystery which moved the

The village and pier, the landing place for modern-day travellers.

83

minds of the old seers and bards. Yonder, where that thin spray quivers against the thyme-set cliff, is the Spouting Cave, where to this day the Mar-Tarbh, dread creature of the sea, swims at the full of the tide. Beyond, out of sight behind these craggy steps, is Port na Curaich, where, a thousand years ago, Columba landed in his coracle. Here, eastward, is the landing-place for the dead of old, brought hence out of Christendom for sacred burial in the Isle of the Saints. All the story of the Gael is here. Iona is the microcosm of the Gaelic world.' – (Fiona Macleod.)

An ancient prophecy attributed to Columba, and cherished by all lovers of Iona, runs as follows:

> *An I mo chridhe, I mo ghràidh,*
> *An àite guth mhanach bidh geum bà;*
> *Ach mu'n tig an savghal gu crìch,*
> *Bithidh I mar a bha.*

> *In Iona of my heart, Iona of my love,*
> *Instead of monk's voice shall be lowing of cows;*
> *But ere the world shall come to an end,*
> *Iona shall be as it was.*

Chapter Ten

MODERN
DEVELOPMENTS

If in the twenties when Marian McNeill wrote the major part of this remarkable history she had needed to travel from Iona to the nearest large city, Glasgow, the journey would have taken her a full day, and in winter almost two.

Today the same journey may be done in five hours.

The effect of this increased accessibility both of the island and the mainland has been considerable and it would be inappropriate to allow a new edition of the work without making reference to the several changes that have taken place on Iona in the intervening years, most of which may be linked to this improvement in transport.

The main change has been the greatly increased number of daily visitors now coming to Iona, with the annual total of inward journeys on the ferry now, in 1990, hovering around the quarter of a million mark, a record which has been surpassed in each of the last four years.

This means that there are now more than two thousand two hundred visitors to the island in ratio to each one of the local residents.

Strangely this vast cargo of human beings has not sunk the local community, nor has it totally ruined Iona's peace, largely because the vast majority of those visitors seem content not to stray beyond the road between the Abbey and the pier or the two tourist restaurants which now do a roaring trade from spring to autumn.

This huge influx has naturally spawned a number of tourist servicing businesses although the local community is still culturally a crofting one.

The facilities include several well equipped boats running day trips to Staffa, two large self-service grocery shops, a pottery, two craft shops and even a facility for hiring pony traps for the island rides.

Most of these tourist facilities are well managed and development is tightly controlled by the National Trust for Scotland who have been the island's partial landlords since 1979.

Soon after the small motor launch that served as a ferry was replaced by a larger island class craft which is capable of carrying far greater numbers of people as well as the cars of local residents and service vehicles.

The island boasts a robust primary school which educates the local children up till the age of eleven, after which they go on to board at Oban and, in a high instance, tertiary education. Sadly the lack of career opportunities and ruinously high cost of housing means that few of the islands children are able to return to live on the island.

The Iona Community – the small discipline of radical Christians, who established their order around the project to restore the ruined Cathedral, has grown beyond its wildest dreams and is now regarded as being at the forefront of innovative work in formalised European Christianity.

The once ruined Cathedral is now completely restored which, together with a forty-bed youth centre serves as both an administrative base for the scattered order and also as a busy residential centre that attracts visitors from around the world for week long visits.

Recently these visitors have included leading members of the armed forces who have come to discuss change with peace campaigners, Church leaders from many different denominations discussing ecumenical progress, and others of many different persuasions from many nations who have come to Iona to rejoice in their shared humanity, and talk, amidst the beauty of the island.

This has brought a new interest in St. Columba's prediction that:

Unto this place, small and mean though it be, great homage shall yet be paid, not only by the kings and peoples of the Scots, but by the rulers of barbarous and distant nations with their people.

The latest ferry to ply its way between Iona and Mull, it replaced a small motor launch, and carries a larger number of people, as well as the cars of local residents and service vehicles.

Sue Anderson

Appendix I

THE NEIGHBOURING ISLES AND STAFFA

The numerous islets lying off Iona are more or less of similar aspect: bird-haunted rocks, grown over with turf and heather, appearing at first sight barren and devoid of interest, but in reality possessing a peculiar charm which only intimate acquaintance can reveal. On a diminutive scale they are full of feature, for nature, whose hand alone has touched them, abhors monotony. Each has its particular view-point of the wide, Hebridean seas and skies. Each, too, has its population, its little life of small, shy creatures that haunt beach and bog and meadow, and, as in the remoter Orkneys, its surface 'is ever beat upon by soft, soundless feet and shadowed by swiftly moving wings, and many a little comedy or tragedy is played out upon its stage. We walk upon it in spring or summer through an air fragrant with the perfume of innumerable small, sweet flowers, with the music of birds and bees about us, and ever under and behind all song, the voice of the great sea, full of undefinable mystery, as of a half-remembered dream' – (Duncan Robertson).

EILEAN CHALMAIN, off the southern extremity of the Ross of Mull, is one of the most charming of these islets, especially in early spring, when it is festive with wild flowers. In autumn it yields a rich harvest of brambles.

EILEAN NAM MUC (Isle of Pigs (? Sea-pigs or Whales)) takes its name from a species of seal that used to haunt its shores. In the month of August the island is white with the heather that is said to bring luck to all finders; but unfortunately the vandals amongst the yearly visitors are reducing the carpet to patchwork.

EILEAN NA H'AON CHAORACH (Island of One Sheep) lies south of Port na-Curaich. The name gives the measure of the islet's pasturage.

IONA – A HISTORY OF THE ISLAND

EILEAN NAM BAN (The Women's Island) lies close to the Mull shore, just opposite to the Iona ruins. To this place, tradition says, Columba banished all women and cows from Iona for a reason preserved in the old distich:

> *Far am bi bo bidh bean,*
> *S' far am bi bean bidh mallachadh.*
>
> *Where there is a cow,*
> *There will be a woman;*
> *And where there is a woman,*
> *There will be mischief.*

Probably the island was set apart for the wives of labourers employed by the monks.

SOA which lies well off the southern shore of Iona, was in early times the monastery seal-farm, which helped to supply the table on fast days. Adamnan relates how a thief named Erc hid on the shore of Mull 'that by night he might sail over to the little island where the sea-calves, ours by right, are bred and breed.' Seals still make their home on the lonely islet, and their movements may be studied here at close quarters.

ERRAID is a larger island – practically an isthmus at low tide – close to the Ross. Robert Louis Stevenson once spent some time on the island, and David Balfour, the hero of his *Kidnapped*, is wrecked on its shore at the beginning of his adventurous journey across the country.

From the high ground of Erraid there is a fine view of the southern isles.

MULL is one of the largest islands in the Hebrides, and is so indented with bays and sea lochs that though its greatest length is only thirty-five miles, its circumference is actually three hundred.

The Ross, or south-western extremity, off which Iona lies, is unimposing in line, but has great beauty of colour. The picturesque hamlets of Fionnphort and Kintra are within easy boating distance, but finer far is the sail through dark Loch Scridain, on the inner side of the rocky headland Bourg, to Pennyghael, whence the road to Salen traverses some of the wildest and grandest country in Scotland. The squalls that descend frequently from the hills to the loch give a spice of adventure to the trip (and, incidentally, call for oilskins). Near the head of the loch, the ascent of Ben More (3097 feet) may be made. This country is the scene of William Black's *Macleod of Dare*.

The outer side of the Bourg is well worth exploring. Myriads of cormorants nest in the shelving rocks, and wild goats wander on the grassy slopes below. A fine cave, known as MacKinnon's, lies a little south of the Isle of Inch Kenneth, where Dr. Johnson and Boswell once spent a night.

Since this book was written the Bourg area, with its famous fossil tree, has come into the care of the National Trust for Scotland. The island, although still sadly empty of people compared with its heyday a hundred and fifty years ago, now has a lively tourist trade of its own for such attractions as the Torosay railway, the Mull Little Theatre and the museum at Tobermory.

The main point of access to Mull, and therefore to Iona and the other islands, is the ferry port of Craignure with several sailings a day from Oban operated by Caledonian MacBrayne. From Craignure there are regular bus services to Tobermory and the Iona ferry at Fionnphort; it is advisable to consult the timetables carefully, especially in winter. There is another, smaller car ferry from Fishnish to Lochaline in Ardnamurchan.

Other islands within reach by open boat – though the remoter ones should be attempted only in the most favourable weather – are Ulva, a name familiar to readers of Campbell's *Lord Ullin's Daughter*; Gometra, close by Ulva; the lonely Treshnish Islands, including the quaintly-shaped Dutchman's Cap; Tiree, closely associated with the ecclesiastical history of Iona; and Staffa, which is described separately.

STAFFA (Stafr-ey, the Isle of Staves or Columns) is a rocky islet about one and half miles in circumference, lying eight miles north of Iona.

In the remote past, the north-west coast of Scotland was the scene of violent volcanic action, which has left traces along the west coast, a line extending from Skye to the Giant's Causeway in Ireland. In consequence of the subterranean disturbances, large volumes of liquid basalt were thrown forth, which, when it began to cool, formed in Staffa, as elsewhere, tiers of columns, curiously symmetrical in shape and size. The action of the waves and the weather throughout the centuries that followed created the amazing caverns of Staffa:

IONA – A HISTORY OF THE ISLAND

Where as to shame the temples decked
by skill of earthly architect,
Nature herself, it seemed, would raise
A Minister to her Maker's praise.
– Sir Walter Scott

Fingal's Cave, the 'Minster' of the above lines, is the largest of the caves, and, as a rule, the only one visited. Its old Gaelic name is 'Uamh Bhinn,' the Melodious Cavern. The grandeur and solemnity of this mighty cavern cannot be fully realised amongst the motley crowd in which the majority of visitors make their approach. 'How could we feel it?' asked Wordsworth; 'each the other's blight':

One votary at will might stand
Gazing, and take into his mind and heart,
With undistracted reverence, the effect
Of these proportions where the Almighty Hand
That made the worlds, the Sovereign Architect,
Had designed to work as if with human Art.

The height of the great arch, at mean tide, is sixty-six feet; the depth of the sea below is about the same; and the cliff above rises a further thirty feet. The length is two hundred and twenty-seven feet – half as much again as that of Iona Abbey Church. The sides, at the entrance, are vertical and nearly parallel, and are composed of black basaltic pillars, of which the majority are pentagonal or hexagonal in form, and divided transversely by joints, like the columns of ancient Greek temples at almost equal distances of two feet. The lights that tremble and flicker over the pillars reveal in the dark basalt warm tints of red and brown and russet; here and there the rock is crusted with gold and green lichen, and the depths of the clear green sea below abound with polyps and the beautiful blue medusae. A constant boom, as of distant thunder, fills the air as the Atlantic swell bursts into the cave, and the voices of the sea-birds ring high and clear above the tumult. Here, one feels, in the ocean solitudes, the elemental forces have hewn a temple of wild and noble splendour, wherein to worship the Power that rules them; and the awed observer perforce bows with them.

'I have seen the temple not made with hands,' wrote Sir Robert Peel,

Alba Pictures

Am Baile Mor, as the village is called in gaelic, another restful scene on Iona.

after a visit to Staffa, 'and have felt the majestic swell of the ocean – the pulsation of the great Atlantic – beating in its inmost sanctuary, and swelling a note of praise nobler far than any that ever pealed from human organ.'

From the landing-place to the top of the island, a stair has formed, and glimpses of the cliffs and caves on the other side of the island may be obtained. The Boat Cave, accessible only by sea, is one hundred and fifty feet long; the Cormorants', or MacKinnon's, is two hundred and twenty feet in length, and fifty in height at the entrance; the Clam Shell is smaller, but is interesting because of its shape, the columns being bent like ship's timbers.

Not far from Fingal's Cave is the Giant's Colonnade – an islet formed of a group of columns about 30 feet high, and well worthy of inspection.

Staffa is now in the care of the National Trust for Scotland. There are regular trips to it by boat, weather permitting, from Iona, Fionnphort and Ulva. In summer it is advisable to make reservations; on fine days in June, July and August there is seldom much room for casual trippers.

CHRONOLOGICAL TABLE

521	Birth of Columba		Martyrs' Bay
563	Columba lands on Iona (12th May)	814	Primacy of Columban Church
574	Columba consecrates Aidan king of		transferred to Kells
	the Scots of Dalriada on Iona – the	825	Martyrdom of St. Blathmac
	first coronation in Britain	844	[Kenneth Mac Alpin, first king of Picts
575	Convention of Drumceatt clarifies		and Scots]
	position of Scots Dalriada	850–900	Early Norwegian settlement in
597	Death of Columba (9th June);		Hebrides
	succeeded as abbot by Baithene	980	Olaf, king of Danes, retires to end his
	[Augustine lands in Kent]		days on Iona
617	St. Drostan and fifty-two monks killed	986	Massacre of the White Sands: abbot
	on the Isle of Eigg at the instigation of		and fifteen monks
	a queen of Picts	1040/1057	Duncan and Macbeth supposedly last
627	[Edwin of Northumbria baptised by		kings buried on Iona
	Paulinus; pagan resurgence after his	c.1070	[Malcolm Canmore marries Saxon
	death in 633; Oswald, educated in		princess Margaret]
	Iona, succeeds in 634]	1097	Bones of Donald Ban reportedly
635	Aidan as missionary from Iona at		reburied on Iona
	Oswald's request founds monastery at	1098	Magnus of Norway visits Iona
	Lindisfarne (Holy Island)	1154	Diocese of Man and the Isles placed in
657–669	Cummian the Fair, seventh abbot,		Province of Nidaros (Trondheim,
	writes On the Virtues of St. Columba		Norway)
664	Synod of Whitby: King Oswiu,	c.1160	St. Oran's Chapel built by Somerled,
	Oswald's successor, adopts Roman		Lord of Argyll
	Church practices		(d. 1164)
679–704	Adamnan, ninth abbot, writes Life of	1164	First mention of Culdees on Iona;
	St. Columba		mission to Ireland
716	Iona monastery adopts Roman Easter	1188	[Pope Clement III declares Scottish
717	Columban monks expelled by Naiton,		Church independent of English]
	king of Picts	c.1200	Reginald, son of Somerled, founds
749	'A great wind. Drowning of the		Benedictine abbey and Augustinian
	Family of Ia' (Irish Chronicle)		nunnery on Iona
c.750	Carving of the Iona High Crosses	1203	Clement III accords Iona community
c.787	Order of Cele De (Culdees) founded in		his special protection
	Ireland	1210	Norwegian saga records raid on 'the
795	Vikings sack Iona		holy island'
802	Vikings burn Iona monastery	1266	Norway cedes Hebrides to the King of
806	Massacre of sixty-eight monks at		Scots

CHRONOLOGICAL TABLE

1314	Angus Og of the Isles with Bruce at Bannockburn
1421–1465	Abbot Dominic, rebuilder of the Abbey
1472	Diocese of the Isles formally transferred from Nidaros
1493	Forefeiture of the Lordship of the Isles
1506	Abbey Church elevated to Cathedral
1549	Donald Monro, Dean of the Isles, describes Iona
1560	[Scottish Reformation] Iona comes under control of MacLeans of Duart
1609	Statutes of Iona
1635	Charles I grants money for restoring Iona Cathedral
1661	Last resident minister until 1828
c.1693	Iona comes under control of Campbells of Argyll
1745	Iona men out with MacLean of Duart for Prince Charles
1772	Pennant visits Iona
1773	Johnson and Boswell visit Iona
1828	'Parliamentary' church and manse
1843	Iona minister, Rev. Donald MacVean, secedes to Free Church at Disruption of Church of Scotland
1874	Eighth Duke of Argyll consolidates Cathedral and other ruins
1899	Duke of Argyll establishes Iona Cathedral Trust 'in connection with' the Established Church of Scotland
1900	[Union of Free and United Presbyterian Churches]
1910	Restoration of Abbey church completed
1927	St. John's Cross patched and re-erected on Iona
1929	[Union of Church of Scotland and United Free Church]
1938	Iona Community founded by Rev. Dr. George F. MacLeod
1940	Chapter house and library restored by Iona Community
1953	Restoration of refectory completed
1955	East range and St. Columba's shrine restored
1956	The Queen, the Duke of Edinburgh and Princess Margaret visit Iona
1957	Restored St. John's Cross falls a second time; Dr. MacLeod, Moderator of the General Assembly of the Church of Scotland; excavators discover what they believe to be St. Columba's cell; St. Oran's Chapel re-roofed
1959	Joint appeal by Community and Cathedral Trustees; restoration of cloisters completed
1961	Michael Chapel opened
1964	Museum completed; memorial stones removed there to avoid further erosion
1965	Restoration completed with rebuilding of west range
1970	St. John's Cross replica erected on original site
1979	Hugh Fraser Foundation buys Iona estate for the nation; now in care of National Trust for Scotland
1988	MacLeod Centre opened
1990	St. John's restoration in converted Abbey museum; Iona Heritage Centre opens in the manse

Appendix III

BIBLIOGRAPHY

During the last few years there has been a great deal of writing about Iona, about Celtic and mediaeval Scotland and about other related subjects. Most imposing is the inventory of antiquities of Iona (Argyll, volume 4) published by the Royal Commission on the Ancient and Historical Monuments of Scotland in 1982. It has a full bibliography.

Other notable publications are the latest edition of Adamnan's *Life of St. Columba*, edited by A.O. and M.O. Anderson (1961), *The Beatons*, by John Bannerman (1981), Ronald Ferguson's history of the Iona Community, *Chasing the Wild Goose* (1988) and of its founder, *George MacLeod, Founder of the Iona Community* (1990), and *Iona, the Living memory of a Crofting Community*, by E. Mairi MacArthur (1990).

General works which make an excellent basis for understanding the role of Iona in history are the first two volumes of the Edinburgh History of Scotland: *The Making of the Kingdom*, by A.A.M. Duncan (1975) and *The Later Middle Ages*, by Ranald Nicholson (1974). *Warlords and Holy Men*, by Alfred P. Smyth (1984) and *Celtic Britain*, by Lloyd Laing (1981) are also good reading with useful bibliographies.

The author's original bibliography, arranged chronologically, is as follows:

c.700   Adamnan (*ob.* 704) – *Vita Sanctae Columbae*. Trans. W. Huyshe. (Routledge's Shiling Library.) Bede (*ob.* 735) – *Opera Historica*. Plummer, 1896.

900–1000   *Irish Life of St. Columba*. Trans. from the Leabhar Breac, in Skene's Celtic Scotland.

1187   [*Chronicles of the Scots and Picts*. Skene's edition, 1867.]

1251   [*Chronicle of the Picts and Scots*. Skene's edition, 1867.]

1400–1500   [*Annals of Ulster*. Ed. by Henessy and Macarthy, 1901.]

1549   Monro's Account in *Macfarlane MSS*. (Advocate's Library). Early MS. in Switzerland.

1600–1700   [*Annals of Ireland by the Four Masters*. Compiled from older sources in the seventeenth century. Ed. by O'Donovan, 1856.]

1702   *Sacheverell* – An Account of the Isle of Man, with a Voyage to Icolmkill in the year 1688.

1703   Martin's Description of Western Isles.

1774   Pennant – *Voyage to the Hebrides*.

1785   Boswell – *Journal of a Tour to the Hebrides with Samuel Johnson* – Carruther's Edition, 1852.

1833–41   Maclean's Historical Account of Iona.

1834   Transactions of Iona Club.

1850   Graham – *Antiquities of Iona*.

1872   Ewing (Bishop) – *Iona*.

1875   Skene – *Notes on the Earlier Establishments at Iona*. In Proceedings of Society of Antiquaries of Scotland, 1875.

1876   Skene – *Notes on the History of the Ruins at Iona*. P.S.A.S., 1876.

1878   Argyll (Duke of) – *Iona*.

1881   Drummond – *Sculptured Monuments in Iona and the Western Highlands*.

1881   [Warren – *Liturgy and Ritual of the Celtic Church*.]

1890   [Skene – *Celtic Scotland*.]

1893   Wilson – *Guide to Staffa and Iona*.

1894   [Dowden – *Celtic Church in Scotland*.]

   [Stephen – *History of the Scottish Church*.]

1896   [McGibbon and Ross – *Ecclesiastical Architecture of Scotland*.]

1898   Macmillan and Brydall – *Iona: Its History and Antiquities*.

BIBLIOGRAPHY

1900   Macleod (Fiona) – *Iona* (with other essays).

1903   [Geikie (A.) – *Text-book of Geology.*]

1904   [Allen – *Celtic Art in Pagan and Christian Times.*]

1909   Trenholme (E. C.) – *The Story of Iona.*

1913   Troup, G. E. – *Monograph, Saint Columba, The Lord's Song in a Strange Land.* Edinburgh, 1913.

1920   Lucy Menzies – *St. Columba of Iona.* (Reprinted 1970).

1928   A. and E. Ritchie – Map of Iona, republished (1964) as 'Iona Past and Present'.

Since 1938 the Iona Community has published the following books and pamphlets about Iona:

Iona: A Book of Photographs.

Murray (Ellen) – *Peace and Adventure: The Story of Iona.*

St. Columba: Fourteenth Centenary

Morrison (John) Editor – *Behold Iona.*

Reece (Richard) – *Iona: Its History and Archaeology.*

Semple (John) – *The Stones of Iona.*

N.B. For further insight into the Celtic spirit, for which Iona stands, the 'Carmina Gadelica,' collected and annotated by Alexander Carmichael, and Campbell's 'Tales of the West Highlands' are of the greatest value, whilst amateurs of art should study in one of the bigger libraries, facsimilis of Celtic manuscripts, such as the Books of Durrow and Kells, and amateurs of music the volumes of ancient songs. 'Songs of the Hebrides' (Boosey & Co.), collected up and down the Isles by Marjorie Kennedy-Fraser (whose ashes lie in Iona) and Kenneth Macleod.

Appendix IV

ISLAND ADDRESSES

Iona Heritage Trust

Secretary:

MRS FREDA ATHERNE,
Roseneath Cottage,
Isle of Iona,
Argyll

National Trust for Scotland

Factor (West):

MICHAEL HUNTER,
Hutchesons' Hall,
158 Ingram Street,
Glasgow G1

Oban Mull and District Tourist Board

Information Centre,

Oban,

Argyll

PA34 4AN

Iona Cathedral Trust

Clerk and Treasurer:

LAWRENCE D. MARDHALL
J&F Anderson WS,
48 Castle Street,
Edinburgh
EH2 3LX

Isle of Iona Community Council

Chairman:

MRS EVELYN MACPHAIL,
Staffa Cottage,
Isle of Iona,
Argyll

Iona Community

Wardens:

REVS.
ALISON AND PHILLIP NEWELL
The Abbey, Isle of Iona,
Argyll PA76 6SN

INDEX